# of Contents

The change in light - its color and atmosphere - always tells me the change of seasons. The light changes before the weather does. One day I notice the light has become softer, and a few days later, a spring storm comes.
The 10th issue of amirisu (we have to celebrate!) showcases a collection that takes in and reflects the delicate light of spring. Not a spring of full brightness, but a warm subtle start of a spring, typical of Japan. Muted colors, intricate details, and a vintage feel. All pieces are versatile and comfortable to wear. We look forward to seeing how you coordinate them with your wardrobe.
The Craft City Guide features Nashville, TN, the city that is quickly becoming a southern hub of crafts and talents. This city with its rich textile history has attracted a lot of aspiring young musicians, and has gradually become a mecca of small businesses, especially in the handmade area. The organic network of creators fuels the energy of the city, making Nashville more attractive to visitors and residents alike. Nashville is also known for its antique market - the vintage atmosphere of which is well suited for this issue's style.
When spring light wakes you up extra early, may this issue of amirisu be a welcome companion over morning coffee.

Tokuko & Meri

光の雰囲気や色の変化を目にするとき、いつも季節の移り変わりを実感します。光の変化は天候の変化よりも先に訪れます。あ、もう春の光だな、と思うと、春の嵐がやってきます。
amirisu の記念すべき 10 号は、そんな春の光を感じさせるコレクションを目指しました。明るさ全開の春ではなく、日本らしい、暖かで密やかな春の始まりです。ちょっとヴィンテージなイメージで、抑えたトーンのグラデーションに繊細なディテール。どれもワードローブで活躍しそうなものばかりだと思います。皆さんにどのように着こなしていただけるか、今から楽しみです。
クラフト・シティ・ガイドではいまアメリカで次のポートランドと目されるナッシュヴィルを紹介。繊維産業が盛んな土地柄に加え、生活費の安さに惹かれてミュージシャンを目指す自由業の若者が多く集まり、次第にスモールビジネスのメッカに成長してきた街です。クリエーターたちがあつまり、お互いの有機的なネットワークによってさらに盛り上がる。そんな雰囲気が感じられます。有名なアンティークマーケットもあって、この号のヴィンテージな雰囲気にぴったりです。
日差しの明るさに早く目覚めた朝、この 1 冊がコーヒーを片手にくつろぐお供になりますように。

トクコ & メリ

An Entry To The Log Book

Artwork courtesy of Shari Altman

Silk & Wool
Premium Yarns Spun in the USA
HD Harrisville Designs
harrisville.com

©MADELINETOSH
HAND DYED YARNS

Local Yarn - Reunion Yarn Company

毛糸紹介：Reunion Yarn Company

Based in Tennessee, Reunion Yarn Company was started by a couple, Emily, who studied textile design, and Michael, who is a trained industrial designer. It's not a typical yarn company. They procure knitwear from secondhand shops, salvage the yarn, and combine different colors and materials to produce totally new yarns.

Throughout her studies, Emily learned the difficulty in creating truly Eco-friendly yarn. Together with Michael, she set up an efficient process to salvage yarns from sweaters. Because commercial knitwear uses very thin yarns, they spin them together so that they become more hand-knitting friendly.

They often set up a booth at Sunday markets in Chattanooga and Porter Flea in Nashville. We hope you get to touch their beautiful yarn in person.

テキスタイル・デザインを専攻したエミリーと、インダストリアルデザイナーのマイケル。米国テネシー州を拠点に夫婦で始めた小さい毛糸メーカーが Reunion Yarn です。毛糸メーカーといっても、糸を作っているわけではありません。リサイクルショップから買ってきたセーターを糸として再生し、色や素材を組み合わせて新しい糸を生み出しているのです。

大学院でサステイナブルなテキスタイル産業のありかたを勉強したエミリーは、完全に環境に優しい毛糸を作る難しさを実感。マイケルとともに既存のセーターを効率よくリサイクルする仕組みを作り出しました。既製品のセーター糸は細すぎるため、手編み用に 2~3 本撚りにしています。

応援したいユニークな試み。今後の展開が楽しみです。

http://www.reunionyarn.com/

Photos by Reunion Yarn Company.

Our Favorites

New lace yarns were released, just in time for the warmer season.
今年お目見えしたレース糸を紹介。

Lace weight yarns are often tightly spun superwash merino and silk, strong but not stretchy. Two new lace-weight yarns recently arrived at amirisu are both two-ply Rambouillet, very springy and soft. The yarns bloom somewhat by blocking, which makes shawls extremely light and airy. Maybe it is time for you to try a large lace shawl.

最近 amirisu が手にした２つの新しいレース糸。これまでレースといえば、スーパーウォッシュやシルク混など、撚りの強いさらっとしたタイプが主流でしたが、今年リリースされた糸はいずれも米国産 Rambouillet 種の２本撚り。もっちりと柔らかく、自然の風合いが魅力です。ブロッキングしたらふわっと軽いショールになりそうで、とてもワクワクします。この春夏はちょっと大判のレースショールにチャレンジしてみたいですね。

Brooklyn Tweed PLAINS

This new yarn from Brooklyn Tweed is a limited edition product only available through their website. It is very light and easy to knit with. The slightly thick and thin character of this yarn adds texture to knit fabric.

BT のウェブサイトで限定販売のレース糸。軽くて編みやすいと評判です。太さにばらつきがあるのが、ナチュラルな感じ。

100% Rambouillet Wool
440 yards (402m) / 50g

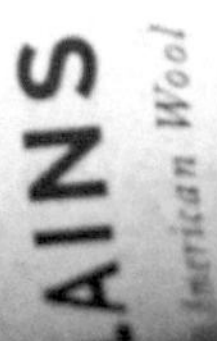

Yarn on the House Mother

A heavy lace-weight yarn with a bouncy, squishy feel. It is close to fingering weight, and is perfect for both shawls and light-weight garments.

Fingering に近い、Heavy Lace Weight のウール糸。太めなので編みやすく、伸縮性は抜群。ショールからウェアまで幅広く使えそうな糸です。

100% Rambouillet Wool
550 yards (503m) / 100 g

Craft City Guide

Nashville, TN

クラフト・シティ・ガイド：ナッシュヴィル

The third Craft City Guide features Nashville, Tennessee, a city that has been attracting artists and makers in recent years. Karen Templer, who moved from the Bay Area a few years ago, and Nashville-native Meg joined us to pick their favorite places, and explore the city.

シリーズ 3 回目は、近年クリエイターたちが集まってきて活気に溢れるテネシー州ナッシュヴィルを紹介。ナッシュヴィルに魅了されて移住したカレンと、メグ (p.16 で紹介) に街のおすすめスポットをピックアップしてもらいました。

When people think of reasons to visit Nashville, they traditionally think of music, not yarn. And they imagine every resident owns a guitar, not a spinning wheel or dye pot. What's becoming increasingly apparent to those outside of Nashville, though, is that it's a town with an amazingly vibrant maker community — and I've discovered that the two things are related. Very often you meet a jeweler or leather crafter or fiber artist, and find out they came to Music City to pursue a music career, but they support themselves through their handmade goods. The fact is, Nashville is a town of creatives.

On the fiber and textiles front, we have more than 150 clothing and accessories designers in Nashville (one of the highest concentrations among US cities), and they're largely focused on local production — even in-house production — and collaboration. For instance, several use fabric that's custom-woven for them right here by weaver Allison Volek-Shelton, of Shutters and Shuttles, who also produces and dyes (and sells) some of the yarn she weaves with.

Moreover, it's a serious yarn town. I moved myself and Fringe Supply Co., my knitting tools-and-accessories business, from Berkeley to Nashville in 2014, attracted by the creative community. At the time, there were two big yarn stores — Haus of Yarn, my ancestral home as a knitter, on the well-established West side; and Bliss, just south of town. In the past year, two more have opened: Craft South in the bustling 12South neighborhood, and Nutmeg in hipster East Nashville. In 2015, Stitches South, the big knitting convention, relocated from Atlanta to Nashville and is now held at Opryland Convention Center each spring. And in the fall, we have the new East Side Fiber Festival put on by Nutmeg, and Fiber in the 'Boro in nearby Murfreesboro, both of which combine regional yarn and fiber companies with fiber animals, demonstrations and more. Not to mention the host of alpaca farms in the region, the countless spinners and dyers, and so many other fibery businesses. We even have a brilliant felting artist, Caleb Groh of Groh Artifact, who creates incredibly expressive mounted animal heads out of roving and batting. (Seriously, google him.)

So whether you're coming for the music scene and want to check out some yarn destinations while you're at it, or you're specifically a textile tourist, there's plenty to see in Nashville. And it's worth noting that you'll eat well while you're here — our restaurant scene is alive and booming.

Text by Karen Templer.

ナッシュヴィルを訪れる理由といえば常に音楽であって、毛糸を思い浮かべる人はあまりいなかったでしょう。この街の住民なら皆ギターを持っているだろう、と想像はしても、紡ぎ車や染色用具を持っているとは考えもしなかったはず。ところが、ナッシュヴィルが驚くほど活気ある工芸作家のコミュニティであるということが、このところ知られるようになってきました。これには 2 つのことが関係しているように思います。ジュエリーデザイナー、レザークラフター、またはテキスタイル・アーティストの多くが、元々はミュージシャンになるためにこの「音楽の街」にやってきたらしいのです。そして、生活のためにモノづくりを始めることに。とにかく、ナッシュヴィルはクリエイティブな人々で溢れています。

テキスタイルや毛糸に関わるところでは、ファッションとアクセサリーのデザイナーが 150 人以上住んでいて、これは米国随一の集積だということ。そして、彼らのほとんどが地元での生産や協業を行っています。たとえば、複数のデザイナーが Shutters and Shuttles を主宰する Allison Volek-Shelton の手織り生地を服地として使っています。(彼女はしばしば自分で糸を紡ぎ染めていて、販売も行っています。)

さらに、ナッシュヴィルは毛糸の街でもあります。自分自身この街のクリエイティブなコミュニティに惹かれ、2014 年にカリフォルニア州バークレーから、Fringe Supply Co. という編みもの道具ショップごと越してきました。引っ越してきた当初、2 つの大きな毛糸ショップがありました。街の西側には House of Yarn という、私の駆け込み寺的毛糸ショップがあり、南に行けば Bliss があります。ところがこの 1 年でさらに 2 つのショップがオープンしました。Craft South は活気ある 12 South 地区に、Nutmeg は最近お洒落度が増している東ナッシュヴィル地区に。毎春開催される Stitches South という大きな編みもののイベントが、2015 年、アトランタからナッシュヴィルに移動してきました。秋には、Nutmeg が主催の East Side Fiber Festival が、近郊 Murfreesboro で行われる Fiber in the 'Boro が、いずれも地域の毛糸や繊維関係の会社を一同に集め、ワークショップやデモンストレーションなども企画されています。そのほか地域にはアルパカ農家、テキスタイルビジネスから趣味の染織家まで、多くが集まっています。面白いものだと、Groh Artifact というフェルト作家が気になっています (ぜひ Google で検索してみてください)。

というわけで、音楽目当てのついでに毛糸ショップに立ち寄るのも、または本気でテキスタイル目当てでも、ナッシュヴィルは見所満載。そして、滞在時は美味しいお店のチェックも忘れずに。グルメでも盛り上がっている街なのです。

カレン・テンプラー

Photo by Talitha Bullock

Rebekka Seale, Camellia Fiber Company

Rebekka Seale is the owner of Camellia Fiber Company, an online shop specializing in handspun and naturally dyed yarn. She was born in Kentucky, raised on the Alabama Gulf coast, and learned to spin yarn and knit as a teenager.

While she was working from home as an illustrator, she started dying yarn and got into natural dyes, which turned into her full-time job. In an effort to sell locally sourced yarn, she started to sell handspun yarn, which is incredibly soft and beautiful.

She is inspired on a daily basis by the rich creative community she became part of in Nashville.

Camellia Fiber Company というブランドで手紡ぎや手染めの毛糸を売るレベッカ。ケンタッキー州生まれ、アラバマ育ち、ティーンエイジャーの頃に紡ぎと編み物を覚えました。

自宅でイラストレーターの仕事をするかたわら、毛糸を染めることにはまり、天然染料に夢中に。家にあまりにも沢山の毛糸が溜まったこともあり、それを仕事にするようになりました。地元ですべてを賄いたいという気持ちから、今は手紡ぎの糸を増やそうと頑張っています。

ナッシュヴィルのクリエイターたちのコミュニティから、日々インスピレーションをもらっているとのこと。

Photo courtesy of the artist.

Allison Volek-Shelton, Shutters and Shuttles

Allison took her first weaving class while she was a student at Tennessee Tech, and has been creating ever since. She got her first loom five years ago, and set up Shutters and Shuttles soon after. In her spacious studio with several looms, she weaves roll after roll of unique textiles, which are primarily sold to local fashion designers.

A very tactile person, she has always been one to reach out and touch things to get a better understanding of them. When she was first introduced to weaving, it was perfect because she could create something meant to be touched.

テネシー工科大学在学中に初めて織りの授業を受け、それ以来ずっと織り続けているというアリソン。5年前に初めて自分の織り機を買い、すぐに Shutters and Shuttels（カメラのシャッターと織りのシャトル）をスタートさせました。現在は広いスタジオを他のクリエイターとシェアし、5、6台はある織り機で大きなロールの生地を創り出しています。そのほとんどは、地元のファッションデザイナーに納品されています。

創作活動ではテクスチャにいつもインスパイアされるとのこと。実際に触って確かめることで、何かを理解するタイプ。大学では陶芸を学んでいたというのも頷けます。テキスタイルという手で触るものを作る仕事は、そんな彼女にぴったりですね。

Meet the Nashville fiber artists ナッシュヴィルのスタジオ訪問

Photo courtesy of the artist.

Anna Maria Horner, Craft South

Energetic and talented Anna Maria is a celebrated textile designer and all-round crafter. Craft South, a yarn and fabric shop opened in 2014, is a handmade heaven. From quilting, dressmaking, needlepoint to knitting, diverse workshops are offered every week. The beautifully and playfully decorated shop has a space for sewing workshops, where you can use their sewing machines and equipment.

Nature and colors inspire her textile design, which she still does by hand drawing and painting.

エネルギーと才能に溢れるアナ・マリアは、大手メーカーからコレクションを出すような有名なテキスタイルデザイナー。刺繍やキルトのキットや本も出しています。そんな彼女が 2014 年にオープンした Craft South は毛糸もファブリックもある、マルチなクラフトショップ。ミシンが沢山並ぶワーキングスペースがあって、そこでキルト、洋裁、ニードルポイントなどのワークショップが毎週開催され、店内はカラフルで楽しい雰囲気があふれています。

デザインをするときは自然や色にインスピレーションをもらうという彼女。コンピューターではなく、すべて手描きで独特な世界を生み出しています。

Photo courtesy of the artist.

Elizabeth Suzann Pape, Fashion Designer

Elizabeth is a self-taught fashion designer, who is probably the most famous among the numbers of Nashville brands. After she spent some years designing and making clothes to sell to local boutiques, she established Elizabeth Suzann in 2013, launched an online retail shop, and is launching a wholesale division.

She is often inspired by stories of the past, and classic style that transcends time and place. She draws ideas from the connections between what is happening in society and fashion, to create timeless pieces that are also comfortable and elegant.

ナッシュヴィルのクリエイターの中で一番有名かつ注目されているのがエリザベス。自分で勉強してファッションデザイナーへの道を切り開きました。しばらくのあいだ地元のブティックなどに作品を卸して生計を立てたあと、2013 年に Elizabeth Suzann というブランドを立ち上げ、現在はオンラインショップでの販売をメインとしています。

デザインの過程では、歴史上の出来事やストーリーに、そして時代を超越したクラシックなスタイルにインスピレーションをもらうとのこと。社会とファッションの接点からアイデアをもらいつつ、長く愛される、そして快適でエレガントなデザインを目指しています。

Photo courtesy of the artist.

Margaret Anderson, Nutmeg

Meg is a Nashville local fiber enthusiast, who realized her dream to open her craft shop in 2014. The cute half-textile, half-yarn shop in East Nashville, Nutmeg, is transitioning into a yarn only shop in 2016.
Her beautifully hand-dyed yarn is one of the key products of the shop, along with Moeke, Brooklyn Tweed and other local yarns.

She finds a lot of inspiration in nature and in her children. She loves to go out and hike, and she spends her time in nature to get ideas and to clear her head for her numerous projects.

ナッシュヴィルで生まれ育ったメグは、ファイバーアーティストとしての夢を実現し、2014年街の東側にNutmegというお店をオープンさせました。これまでファブリックと毛糸と半々に扱ってきましたが、今年毛糸ショップとしてリニューアルする予定なのだとか。自宅で手染めしたオリジナルの毛糸のほか、Moeke や Brooklyn Tweed、そしてその他の地元の毛糸などを扱っています。

自然や子供達から沢山のインスピレーションをもらうというメグ。ハイキングに行ったり、ただ自然の中で過ごすうちに、アイデアが浮かんできたり頭をすっきりさせたりできるそう。

Things to do in Nashville...

For fiber folk, a day in Nashville is not nearly enough, and here is why - there are markets to explore in addition to many exquisite shops and restaurants! Upon planning a trip to Music City, mark these events on your calendar.

ナッシュヴィルを訪れるのに、1日ではまったく足りません。ユニークなお店や美味しいレストランだけではなく、必見のマーケットがあるから。旅を計画する前に、まずこれらのイベントをカレンダーに書き込みましょう。

Flea Market

The flea market in Nashville is one of the biggest and best in the country, which takes place on the fourth weekend of every month (except December). There are approximately 2000 booths set up, coming from all over the country, and it is definitely a place to check out if you are lucky enough to be in town.

ナッシュヴィルのフリーマーケットはアメリカでも最大規模、とても有名なのです。12月を除き、毎月4週目の週末に開催されるこのイベント、全米から2000ほどのブースが集まります。

http://www.thefairgrounds.com/fleamarket/index.asp

Above: photo by Karen Templer.
Below: courtesy of East Side Fiber Festival website.

Stitches South

Stitches events are organized by XRX Inc., a knitting book and magazine publisher in the States. Last year they moved the Stitches South event from Atlanta to Nashville, which suggests the city is becoming the fiber capital of the South. There are dozens of workshops and events to enjoy, as well as the market to explore. The entrance fee to the market is $10 for one day. This year's event is over by the time this issue comes out, but spring time is definitely a time to visit Nashville!

http://www.knittinguniverse.com/South2016

XRXという編み物系の出版社が全米で開催しているStitchesというイベント。これまでStitches Southはアトランタ開催だったのが、昨年からナッシュヴィルに移動してきました。ナッシュヴィルがファイバーアートのメッカになりつつあるのが伺えますね。

棒針とかぎ針のワークショップが多数開催されるだけではなく、沢山のショップも集結。マーケットに入るだけなら、入場料10ドルです。

残念ながら今年のイベントはこの号が出る直前。でも、春はナッシュヴィル訪問に最適な時期であることは間違いありません。

East Side Fiber Festival

Founded by Meg of Nutmeg in 2015, this local fiber festival brings together farmers and artists from Tennessee. The 2016 event is scheduled for September 24th. Visit the website for details.

Nutmegのメグが2015年から始めたイベント、テネシー中からアーティストや生産者が集まります。今年は9月24日の予定。

http://www.eastsidefiberfestival.com/

Yarn Shops | 毛糸ショップめぐり

Nashville has wonderful yarn stores. When in town, please take advantage of them to see quality yarns in person!
ナッシュヴィルは小さな街ですが、いい毛糸屋が揃ってます。ぜひ色々な毛糸に触れてみてください。

Haus of Yarn

They have so much yarn! The sheer amount of quality yarn stock made us envious.
信じられないほどの在庫が。良い糸が本当に揃っています。
265 White Bridge Rd, Nashville, TN 37209
http://www.hausofyarn.com/

Craft South

This beautiful shop, owned by Anna Maria, has both bolts of fabrics and selected brands of yarn. They are the flagship to Quince & Co. and carry Koigu, Sincere Sheep and Camellia Fiber Company yarn.
Anna Maria が経営するこのショップ、ファブリックと毛糸両方が。Quince & Co. や Sincere Sheep の取り扱いのほか、Camellia Fiber Company の糸もあります。
2516 12th Ave S, Nashville, TN 37204
http://www.craft-south.com/

Nutmeg

Meg's shop is small, yet bursting its seams with cute goodies! She carries brands such as Nutmeg and Moeke, and icelanding yarns.
小さいけれど可愛いものがぎっしり詰まったお店。オリジナル糸ほか、Moeke や Lopi などを扱います。
1006 Fatherland St., Ste 204 Nashville, TN 37206
http://www.nutmegster.com/

Bliss Yarns

This shop has an extensive selection of yarns from brands such as Cascade and Schaefer. A favorite shop for local knitters.
Cascade や Schaefer などが充実する、地元ニッターお気に入りのお店。
127 Franklin Rd, Brentwood, TN 37027
http://www.blissyarns.com/

Textiles and Fashion | ファッションとテキスタイル

Shutters and Shuttles

This location is mostly Allison's studio, but you can buy her textiles, clothings and hand dyed yarn.
スタジオスペースが主ですが、手織りの美しいテキスタイル、ウェアや手染めの糸も買えます。
2517 Eugenia Ave, Nashville, TN 37211
http://www.shuttersandshuttles.com/

Jamie & The Jones

Fashion designers who use Allison's textiles. They also share a studio space.
アリソンのファブリックを使って洋服をデザイン。スタジオもシェアしています。
2517 Eugenia Ave, Nashville, TN 37211
http://www.jamieandthejones.com/

Elizabeth Suzann

They accept studio tours by appointments. It's definitely a thing to do in Nashville!
予約制でスタジオの見学ができます（買い物も。）ナッシュヴィルに行くなら是非！
441 Atlas Drive, Nashville, TN 37211
http://elizabethsuzann.com/

Other Crafts | その他のクラフト

Handmade Studio TN

A beautiful shop that sells handmade pottery. There are scheduled workshops as well.
素敵な手作りの器が買えるお店。定期的にワークショップも開催されているので、ウェブサイトをチェック。
100 Taylor Street Studio A23, Nashville, TN 37208
http://www.handmadestudiotn.com/

Hatch Show Print

A historic letter press studio founded in 1875. You can book tours to see prints and machines from the 19th century.
1875 年創業のレタープレススタジオ。予約制のツアーでは、現存する機械や 100 年前の印刷物などに触れられます。
224 5th Ave S, Nashville, TN 37203
http://hatchshowprint.com/

Hey Rooster

A select shop that also hosts craft workshops.
クラフトのワークショップも時々開催する、キュートなセレクトショップ。
1106 Gallatin Avenue Nashville, TN 37206
http://www.heyrooster.com/clayshop/

Printable maps can be downloaded at our blog

地図は amirisu ブログからダウンロードできます

Plaza Art

A local art supply chain where you can take art classes.
地元の画材ショップチェーンで、アートクラスも受講できます。
633 Middleton Street, Nashville, TN 37203
http://www.plazaart.com/classes-workshops/

SmART Supplies

A place where you can find repurposed art supplies, fabric, yarn and more for very cheap!

リサイクルされた画材、ファブリック、糸などが激安で売られています。
4 Buchi Court, Nashville, TN 37204
http://www.smartsupplies.org/

Textile Fabrics

A go-to shop for people looking for good fashion fabrics.
洋裁用のファブリックを買いたいときには外せないお店。品揃え豊富。
471 Craighead Street, Nashville, TN 37204
http://www.textilefabricstore.com/

Turnip Green Creative Reuse

A wonderful community of people that teach classes and workshops. Their focus is on nurturing creativity through reuse of items.
リユースを推進しながら、アートやクラフトのクラスを開催しているコミュニティ。
535 4th Ave. South, Nashville, TN 37210
http://turnipgreencreativereuse.org/

Fort Houston

Studio spaces for rent for artists and makers. It is on a membership basis, and aims to provide a facility for welding, woodworking, and such.
アーティストやクラフト愛好家たちにスペース貸しをしています。溶接や木工の設備も整っていて、楽しい場所。
500 Houston St, Nashville, TN 37203,
http://forthouston.com/

Jill Draper Makes Stuff
hand dyed with love
in the Hudson Valley
jilldraper.com
yarns made sheep to skein in the US

woolfolk
FÅR
WOOLFOLKYARN.COM

Nature's
Luxury
Hand-dyed yarns de luxe
www.naturesluxury.com

Hand Dyed Yarns
www.julie-asselin.com

Spring
Vintage

Sumire

Nadia Crétin-Léchenne

An elegant top down shawl, knit in pale purple and white. A garter stitch border with picot bind off in contrasting color adorns this simple lace shawl. It's a perfect piece for spring strolls.
薄紫のレースに白のボーダーを組み合わせた、エレガントなトップダウン・ショール。シンプルなレースですが、コントラストカラーで編むガーター編みのボーダーとピコット BO で可愛さをプラスしています。春のお出かけのお供にどうぞ。

Kirsten Johnstone

Keshi

Kirsten Johnstone

A tank designed with Shibui Linen and Silk Cloud. While back panel is knit in linen, front panel uses linen and mohair; the combination creates interesting texture and drape. It is a comfortable top to wear from spring through summer.

Shibui Linen と Silk Cloud を合わせたトップス。後ろ身頃はリネンのみ、前身頃はリネン + モヘアの組み合わせを編むことで、異なる質感や光沢を表現しています。形はシンプルなので着やすさは抜群。初夏まで使えそうな 1 枚です。

Sango

Melissa LaBarre

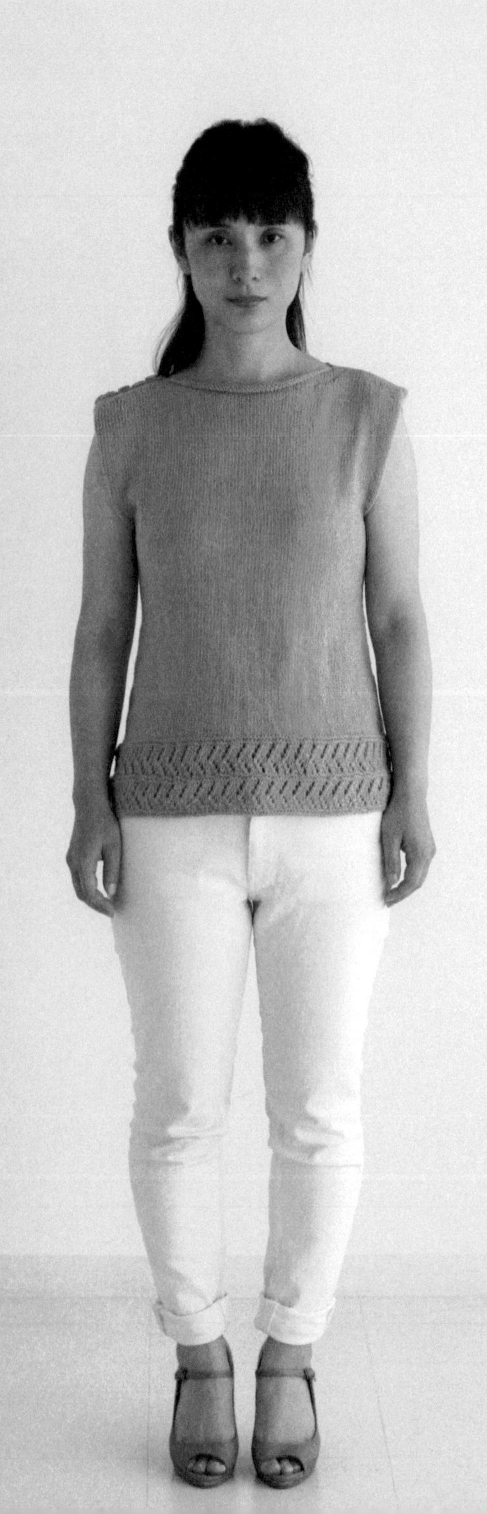

A cotton tee in Quince & Co. Willet, with lovely details including a lace border and shoulder buttons. It's simply shaped so even the sweet pastel colors of Willet won't make it too feminine. A perfect project for a beginner knitter.

Willet で編む、コットンのトップス。裾に入ったレース模様と肩のボタンが可愛いディテールになっています。形がシンプルな分、Willet の柔らかい色合いが映える 1 枚に。ウェア初心者にピッタリな夏まで使える 1 枚です。

Sango

Melissa LaBarre

Camellia

Joji Locatelli

Camellia

Joji Locatelli

Camellia is a drop-sleeve pullover knit in Quince & Co. Finch. It looks like a simple pullover, but to accommodate the strips in the center, Joji has come up with a unique construction. The strips also make the relaxed silhouette look more sophisticated and refined. A great project for intermediate knitters, or for beginner knitters who want to try a challenge.
Finch で編むドロップスリーブのプルオーバー。見た目はシンプルながら、前後に入るストライプを横に編み、身頃を肩から裾に向けて編んだ後、ストライプと合体させる面白い構造になっています。少しゆったり目のシルエットですがストライプのおかげですっきり見えるのもポイント。ちょっとチャレンジしてみたい初級ニッターさんにぴったりの作品です。

Nadeshiko

Leila Raabe

Nadeshiko

Leila Raabe

A crescent-shaped shawl knit in Quince & Co. Piper. After you knit a fan shape with simple stockinette with purl ridges, the fun lace part begins. The lace pattern is simple enough for beginners but creates delicate drape, especially with the soft mohair yarn. It makes a great companion for chilly spring evenings.

Piper で編む半月型のショール。最初は簡単な模様編みを編みながら目を増やしていき、最後のお楽しみとしてレース模様が待っています。初心者にも編みやすい、覚えやすい模様でありながら、モヘアの柔らかさも相まって美しいドレープを作り出します。普段モヘアを敬遠しがちな方にもオススメ。少し肌寒い春の夜のお供に。

Wisteria

Amy Christoffers

This cotton cardigan is perfect for spring weather. Although the garment is knit in lace pattern, the thicker cotton yarn keeps it casual. The lace pattern is simple enough to remember after a few repeats, and the rest is easy. It is a lovely piece for relaxing at home and more formal occasions.
コットンの糸で編む、春にピッタリのカーディガン。総レース模様ですが、少し太めの糸なので甘すぎずカジュアルに着られます。シンプルな模様の繰り返しで、模様を覚えてしまえばスイスイ編み進むはず。日常の羽織物にも、ちゃんとしたお出かけにも使える頼れる１枚になりそうです。

Wisteria

Amy Christoffers

Botan

Helen Stewart

Botan

Helen Stewart

A shawl adorned with bobbles and picots, mostly knit in garter stitch, which makes it a great project for beginner knitters. It makes a lovely spring shawl when knit in cheerful colors like the sample, or knit in neutral colors to make it wearable year-round.
ボッブルとピコットがポイントのショール。ストライプが入りますが、ベースは全てガーター編みの簡単な模様なので、ショール初心者にもピッタリです。サンプルのように春らしい甘い色合いで編んでもかわいいですし、通年使えるように渋めの色合いで編んでも素敵。お好きな色の組み合わせを選んでくださいね。

Asagi

Bristol Ivy

A sweet summer top with lace panels on both shoulders, knit in beautiful spring green Esopus. V-shaped neckline neutralizes the sweetness a little bit, and makes the tee more casual for daily wear. Its interesting construction will keep you entertained throughout the project.

Esopus で編む、袖のレース模様が可憐な半袖プルオーバー。レース模様の甘さを V ネックのシェープで引き締めています。変形トップダウンで、編み方も面白いんですよ。手染め糸の爽やかなアサギ色で春を楽しんで。

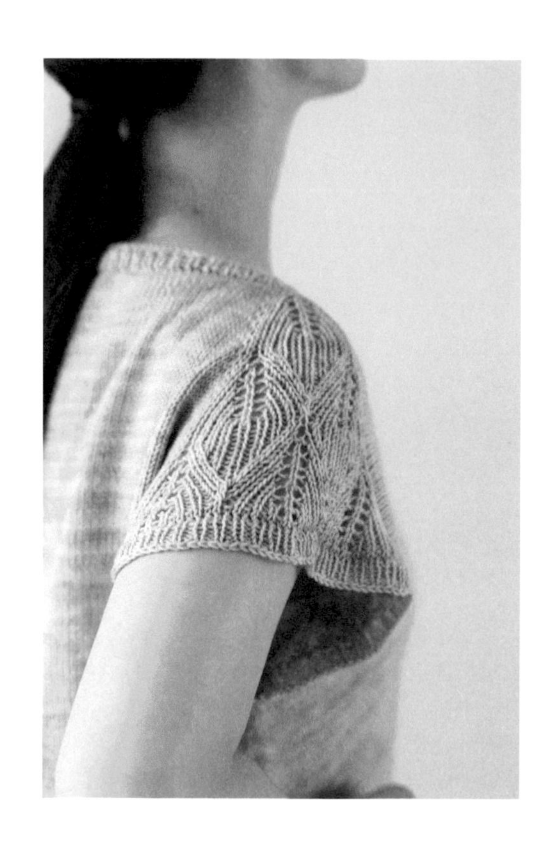

Tools of the Trade

Text by Leila Raabe, Knitwear Designer
レイラの編み物道具紹介

Photo by Leila Raabe

I've pared down my essential knitting kit over the years. Compartments, however, is the name of the game for me. You can never have too many pouches to carry things in. And the right shape and size make a difference! My favorite one is a zippered utility pouch from Forestbound, made from recycled feed sack cotton, with a wide bottom that gives enough room to carry a small WIP. Sometimes I'll use a slimmer pouch like the grey and natural checked one from Fog Linen. Larger projects go in a simple cotton drawstring bag. My small group of tools get their own pouch so everything stays orderly inside whatever bag/purse I head out with for the day. Lately I've been testing smaller-sized ones, like the red and dark grey wool felt pouches from Twig & Horn (these are prototypes for a new item Twig & Horn will be launching soon!) for housing things like my interchangeable circular needles. A smooth, sturdy zipper that opens easily but stands up to a lot of opening and closing is essential. They also need to be lined and durable enough to hold sharp, pointy tools like scissors. Other tools I always carry with me: an adorable wooden acorn stitch marker holder to hold my favorite stitch markers, coil-less pins in different finishes; my favorite portable needle gauge, made of wood and shaped like a bird, a gift from a dear friend; my trusty, bright orange tape measure which is both indestructible and easy to spot when I inevitably set it down among a pile of yarn and books.

道具類は年を追うごとに必要最小限にまとまってきました。すべてを分別してしまうのが好きなので、とにかくたくさんのポーチを持っています。大きさや形がぴったりくると、とてもスッキリするもの。Forestbound のジッパーポーチはリサイクルコットン製、底が幅広で小さい編みかけプロジェクトを持ち運ぶのにお気に入り。小さいプロジェクトには Fog Linen のチェックのポーチを使うことも、大きなものは巾着に入れて持ち運びます。

小さい道具類はそれぞれケースが決まっていて、出かけるときにもバッグのなかで整理整頓されるようになっています。近頃は Twig & Horn のプロトタイプ、フェルトのジッパーバッグを試用しているところ。付け替え輪針や先のとがったものを入れていますが、それには口が広くて、丈夫な裏地のついたポーチが最適。

そのほかいつも持ち歩いているのは、可愛らしい木製のドングリケースと段数マーカー、友達に貰ったお気に入りのニードルゲージ、そして毛糸の山の中からでもすぐに見つかるオレンジ色の巻尺です。

From Our Knitting Classroom

Vol.2 "Excuse me, but I don't know how many rows I should knit."
編み物教室の現場から Vol. 2「先生、結局私は何段編めばいいんですか」
Text by Tokuko

It seems many knitters outside Japan think Japanese knitting patterns are cool and clever. It is true that in some cases Japanese patterns are easier to understand, although it requires some knowledge.

There are many interesting features in Japanese patterns, and one of them is that row counts are indicated in the schematics.

English patterns usually say "work to your desired length" or "continue until the piece measures this length". In Japanese patterns, row counts are usually given alongside with the schematic lengths. This is probably why Japanese students often want to know how many rows they should knit.

Now, think about it. When you are knitting a garment top down or bottom up, you don't have to worry about seaming, nor matching the lengths of front and back, you can work as much body length as you like. You can follow the pattern, or can lengthen or shorten it.

But somehow this is difficult to a lot of Japanese knitters. People almost always want to knit exactly as the sample, and they often tell me that they need to know the row count.

Think about how designers design garments. They always start with length, then calculate how many rows you must knit based on a given gauge. What they want is the finished size they have designed.

This is why some English knitters only check stitch gauge without knitting enough rows. I often do this myself (note: this is only recommended to a skilled knitters who knows their gauge and how the fabrics behave well.)

There are, of course, cases where row gauge is critical. For example, when you knit sweaters horizontally from sleeve to sleeve, you have to know exactly how many rows you need to knit. The other case is when you use materials that are easy to stretch, such as silk blends. You need to check your row gauge and figure out how much the fabric will stretch. This is a little tricky.

The last word - the most important thing is how long the fabric will end up, not how many rows you knit. Please measure your projects frequently.

日本の編み図がクールでクレバーだと思っている外国の方、たくさんいますよね。もちろん日本人にとっても、日本式の方がわかりやすいパターンもあります。読み解くには少し知識が必要なのが残念ですが。

そんな日本の編み図には色々面白い特徴がありますが、そのひとつとして、通常編む段数が明記されているという点があげられます。

英語パターンにある「好きな長さで」や「何 cm まで編む」などの記載はありません。スキーム図の cm 表記の脇には段数が書かれているんです。そのせいか、日本人の生徒さんはとにかく長さではなく何段編むべきかを気にします。

では段数問題について、よく考えてみましょう。例えばトップダウンの場合、ボトムアップの場合など綴じはぎが関係ない場面では好きな長さを編めばいいですよね。段数が後々関係することは全くありません。好きな長さまで編んでもよし、書いてある長さを守ってもよし。段数ではなく長さが問題！

でも、難しいんですよね。とにかくサンプル通りに編みたい願望が強いので、段数を指定してくれないと心配ですという声が聞こえてきそうです。

そこでもうひとつアドバイスを。段数についてデザイナー目線で考えてみましょう。デザイナーがまず考えるのは欲しい長さなんです。長さがあって、それをゲージで計算した結果が段数なんです。段数は後から計算された事実でしかない。ほら、安心したでしょう。その長ささえ出せれば、デザイナーとしては満足なわけですよ。英語圏に目数のゲージはきっちりとっても、段数のゲージは編みながら取っちゃう人がいるのはこのせいです。かく言う私もこの手をよく使います。(注意：自分のゲージや素材の性質を把握している上級者のみオススメです。)

でも、もちろん段数ゲージが大事な場合もあります。たとえばセーターなどを横に編んでいくもの。編んだ段数がそのまま幅になりますので、これは必ずゲージの確認が必要です。あとは、伸びやすい素材のもの。シルク混やアルパカ糸は糸の重みでどうしてもゲージより長くなりがちです。ゲージを取ってみて、さらにそこからどのくらい伸びるかを考えて編まないといけません。なかなか一筋縄ではいきませんが、とにかく言える事はひとつ。段数よりも実際の長さが大事。ゲージを取ったからと安心せずに、編みながら何度も測って下さいね。

Bookish.

CAPSULE

Olga Buraya-Kefelian for Brooklyn Tweed

Softcover, 128 pages. $30.00

Olga's second printed book came out from Brooklyn Tweed last winter. It is a beautifully designed book that reflects both Olga's modern look and Brooklyn Tweed's classic style.

I had been hearing about the book from Olga for a few years, and listened to her worries that the patterns may look outdated. Her worries were needless. All eight patterns in this book are timeless yet current, and I believe they work for all age groups.

While the Jujika cowl (top right photo) is my absolute favorite, with infinite color possibilities, patterns like the Cusp poncho (on the cover), Tatara mitts and Apex cardigan have enough interesting features to keep knitters entertained throughout the projects.

It amazes me how the designer highlighted the potential of the brand's two yarns. Light-weight, woolen-spun Shelter can create a three dimensional effect when knit in a tight gauge. This detail is used effectively in patterns such as Nobu and Tatara. Loft is even lighter yet holds up well, making Apex wearable without stretching like crazy. I know Olga, and I know that she makes these choices intentionally.

Beautifully photographed by Jared Flood, this book is sure to become a treasure in your library.

CAPSULE

著者 : オルガ・ブラヤ=ケフェリアン

ソフトカバー、128 ページ、3,200 円

オルガの 2 冊目の著作が昨年の冬に Brooklyn Tweed からリリースされました。BT のクラシックなスタイルに、オルガのモードな雰囲気がミックスされた、とても美しい本です。

何年も前から計画されていたこの本、なかなか出ないので「もう時代遅れじゃないかしら」という心配も聞いていました。でも心配は無用でした。どのパターンも流行に関係なく、世代に関係なく身につけられるものばかり。

Jujika というカウル (写真右)、色の組み合わせが楽しめそうで特に気に入っていますが、Cusp ポンチョ (表紙)、Tatara リストウォーマー、そして Apex カーディガンなど、構造が面白くて最後まで楽しんで編めそうなパターンばかりです。

パターンがいくつあるのだろう、というくらいデザインされ尽くした Brooklyn Tweed の SHELTER と LOFT ですが、この糸の特性を生かしたさらに新しいデザインを生み出す力に感心です。軽い紡毛糸の SHELTER、きついゲージで編むと立体感が出るのを活かし、Nobu セーターや Tatara などがデザインされています。非常に軽くて編み地がまったくだれない LOFT、Apex のような大きなカーディガンでも着やすいものが出来上がります。普通の糸で編んだら伸びて大変なことになりそう。意図的にデザインと糸の特性をうまく組み合わせているのが伺えます。

ジャレッドが撮った、ブルックリンの美しい写真も見所。本棚の宝物になりそう。

When we came to Vermont, we were lucky to move next door to a beekeeper. He encouraged us to start our own hives and mentored us every step of the way. My husband and I have had honeybees ever since. In the spring, it's exciting to see the bees emerge from the hive after the long winter. We know the bees look for the red maple blooms first in early spring and that they will all congregate on the cherry tree when it blooms, creating quite a hum. In the summer, it's asters and clover. In the fall, goldenrod is king. Being a beekeeper has made us both more aware of the cycles of the natural world.

Shari Altman

ヴァーモント州に引っ越して来た当初、養蜂家とお隣どうしになるという幸運に恵まれました。自分たちで蜂を飼うことを勧められ、手取り足取り指導してくれました。それ以来ずっと、我が家ではミツバチを飼っています。春になると、長い冬のあいだ篭っていた蜂が巣から出てくるのを見て心踊ります。早春はレッドメープルの花を求めて飛び回り、チェリーの花が咲くとそれに音をたてて群がる、そんなことを知りました。夏はアスターとクローバー、秋はキリンソウがなによりのご馳走。蜂飼いになって、自然のサイクルにとても敏感になったわたしたちです。

シャリ・アルトマン

Through the Lens

Shari is a photographer and blogger who lives in Vermont. She contributes a photo journal to this magazine.

シャリはヴァーモント在住のフォトグラファー、ブロガー。毎号 amirisu にフォト日記を寄稿しています。

Contributors

Amy Christoffers

Amy Christoffers is Design Director at Berroco, the author of New American Knits and the designer of Savory Knitting Patterns.

米国大手毛糸メーカー、Berroco のデザイン・ディレクターとして活躍する傍ら、Savory Knitting としてデザイン活動を行う。著書に *New American Knits* がある。

Ravelry: Savory Knitting
savoryknitting.com
www.Berroco.com

Bristol Ivy

Bristol is a knitting designer and fiber artist from Portland, Maine. Her work focuses on the intersection between classic tailoring and innovative technique, creating a unique and wearable aesthetic that's still fun to knit.

メイン州ポートランド在住のニットウェア・デザイナー、ファイバーアーティスト。クラッシックなライン、新しい技法、着やすく個性的なデザイン、編む楽しさを盛り込みつつ、デザインを行う。

Ravelry: BristolIvy
www.bristolivy.com

Leila Raabe

Leila lives in Portland, Maine, loving the versatility of New England life and working with the brilliant minds at Quince & Co. Leila's favorite kind of knitting is tactile, textural, and able to stand the test of time. She can never resist the siren calls of intricate lace for very long.

メイン州ポートランド在住、ニューイングランドでの暮らしと、Quince&Co.での仕事を楽しむ。テクスチャに富んだ長く楽しめる、特にレースをデザインするのが好き。

Ravelry: wolletron
leilaknits.com
Instagram: @leilaknitsme

Joji Locatelli

Joji enjoys living her life in sunny Buenos Aires, while dreaming of visiting the rest of the world armed with knitting needles and yarn. She also thinks life is much sweeter when served with coffee and chocolate...

天気の良いブエノスアイレスでの暮らしを楽しみつつ、編み物と共に世界中を旅することを夢見る。チョコレートとコーヒーがあれば、人生はさらにバラ色に。

Ravelry:jojilocat
www.jojiknits.com

Helen Stewart

Helen lives in London, where she design and host the award-winning Curious Handmade podcast. Helen loves to combine knitting with her other passions - travel, photography and meeting up with knitters around the world.

ロンドン在住、デザイナーとして活動する傍ら、受賞歴もある Podcast、Curious Handmade を運営。編み物と趣味の旅行や写真を組み合わせ、そして世界中のニッターと出会うのが楽しみ。

Ravelry:HellsBells
www.curioushandmade.com

Melissa LaBarre

Melissa is a freelance designer and co-author of the Wool series for Quince & Co., New England Knits, Weekend Hats. Her designs have also been widely published from magazines and yarn companies. She lives with her husband and 2 young children in Massachusetts.

Quince の Wool シリーズや New England Knits などの著作をもつフリーランスデザイナー。雑誌や糸メーカーから幅広く作品を発表している。マサチューセッツ州に夫と子供と暮らしている。

Ravelry: knittingdropout
knittingschooldropout.com

Nadia Crétin-Léchenne

Nadia loves nothing more than having wool between her fingers. She has been a compulsive knitter since childhood. Her daily routine includes some quiet hours, spent dreaming about yarn and designs, with a cup of coffee nearby. She lives in a tiny village in Switzerland, with her husband and six children.

ウールを触るのが何よりも好きで、子供時代より編み物中毒に。コーヒーを手に毛糸やデザインを夢想する静かな時間を大切にする。スイスの村に夫と６人の子供と暮らす。

Ravelry: ittybitty
www.nclknits.com

Kirstin Johnstone

Kirsten is a practicing architect from Melbourne, Australia and she loves to explore her modern aesthetic across a broad range of design disciplines. Kirsten has an eye for flattering forms that are deceptively simple with a stunning attention to detail. Her garments have a distinctive urban edge yet elegantly wearable.

オーストラリアのメルボルンで建築業の傍ら、現代的なデザインをジャンルに関係なく楽しむ。シンプルに見え、着る人を美しく見せるフォルムを目指す。都会的でかつ着やすいデザインをする。

Ravelry: assemblage
kirstenjohnstone.com

Karen Templer

Karen Templer blogs daily about the world of knitting at Fringe Association, while also running Fringe Supply Co. (fringesupplyco.com), and knitting as much as she possibly can.

ウェブサイト Fringe Association を通じ編みものに関する情報を日々発信するかたわら、Fringe Supply Co. という道具ショップを運営。暇を見つけては編みものにいそしむ。

Ravelry: karentempler
fringeassociation.com

Clockwise from the front row left, Ayumi (model), Yoko Yoshikawa (hair and makeup), Ritsue (model), Eri (styling), Masahiro Kohda (photographer), Meri, Tokuko, and Nao (model).

前列左より時計回りに、アユミ（モデル）、吉川陽子（ヘアメイク）、リツエ (モデル)、エリ(スタイリング)、コーダマサヒロ(フォトグラファー)、メリ、トクコ、ナオ(モデル)。

amirisu is:

Tokuko Ochiai オチアイトクコ

Tokuko is a knitwear designer and the co-representative of amirisu co., working non-stop to manage a yarn shop and knitting classes. She finally got used to all her finished projects being taken from her as shop samples. She just moved to Nara.

ニットデザイナー、amirisuの共同代表として毛糸屋運営や教育に全力疾走する毎日。何を編んでも店のサンプルに取られるため、自分の編み物は全くできなくなったことにやっと慣れたところ。昨年から住居を奈良に移し、相変わらず移動し続ける人生を送っている。

Website: KNIT WORK Kemukujyara (http://kemukujyara.p2.bindsite.jp) | Ravelry: tokuko

Meri Tanaka タナカメリ

Meri, the editor, creative and business development director of amirisu co., recently moved to the sacred city of Kyoto. She also works as a freelance translator, specializing in crafts and business areas. Past experience includes a+u magazine, management consulting and marketing.

2014年夏より京都在住。編集業・経営コンサル・マーケティング職を経て、amirisuで編集、クリエティブ・ディレクション、企画等を担当。ビジネスやクラフト関連の通訳・翻訳業も行っている。

Blog: Sparkles*United (http://sparklesunited.com/)
Ravelry: sparklink02

When I had an editorial job at a monthly magazine, we used to work in a team of seven, hence, all the work was devided by seven, and each month's release was sort of like finishing a sweater or shawl. I loved the sense of achievement I felt, when I used to hold freshly printed magazines. After two years had passed, I realized that I had repeated the same process 24 times, and would be repeating it 300 times more. I left the job a month later.

Now I find myself making a magazine again, and this time we started with just two of us, and each release feels like climbing the Alps or Everest to me. We prepare for over six months, and sink everything we've got into reaching our goal. This Fall 2016 issue is our 10th issue. Tokuko and I have climbed 10 majestic mountains and survived. While the act of climbing may stay the same, we feel different, are different, and see different scenes. Our bond has become stronger, and the team has grown.

I look forward to climbing the next 10 mountains, while knitting and connecting with more people. Thank you for your continued support!

かつて月刊誌で働いていたころ、7人程度のチームで役割分担をしていたこともあり、毎月雑誌を出すのはいわばセーターやショールを1つ完成させる感じに似ていました。自分たちで作った本を手にするという達成感。そのうち2年経ったとき、同じ作業を24回繰り返した自分にハッとし、それからさらに240回繰り返す未来を想像し、会社を去ることを決めました。

気がつけば今度はたった2人で、再び雑誌を作る仕事をはじめたわけですが、毎号リリースまでの道のりはアルプスやエベレスト級の山に登るような、自分の中のイメージとしてはそんな感じです。半年かけて準備をし、全力を出しきって作りあげます。今回で10号目、トクコさんと10個の山に登って生きて帰ってきたような気がします。同じ山に登っているようでいて、そのたびに自分たちのありかたも、心持ちも、そして見える景色も違っています。作業を通して私たちの絆は深まり、チームと呼べる人の輪も広がってきました。

次の10号もコツコツと山に登りながら、すてきな編みものの景色を、そのときの自分たちのありかたを楽しみたいと思います。応援をよろしくお願いします！

Meri Tanaka

Reviewing the first issue of amirisu that Meri had republished the other day, made me feel very nostalgic. It also reminded me of how desperate and uncertain I was, and I couldn't help but smile. After a small launch party, I couldn't find the energy to walk home from the station. I finally collapsed in a cab, and started crying. It feels just like yesterday.

With each issue, our pattern editing skill improved, and now I have two wonderful team members to work with. Meri, who has to do everything on her part all by herself, is envious of the team! It is a tough job editing and creating both English and Japanese patterns simultaneously, and all of us work very hard for that. At each release, saying to each other "great job!" still brings me close to tears.

Creating knitwear patterns is a group effort. I hope to involve as many people as possible to get to the next goal. Meri, congratulations on the 10th issue!

先日、メリさんがレイアウトをし直してくれた1号の内容を久しぶりに見て、とても懐かしく、とともにその頃の自分の必死さと未熟さを思い出し、ひとりで苦笑しました。小さな1号リリース記念パーティーの後、帰りの駅から家に帰るまでのたった15分を歩く気力もなく、諦めて乗ったタクシーの中で本当にホッとして、ひっそりと涙をこぼしたことを昨日のように思い出します。号を重ねるごとにパターンを作る技術もあがり、今や私には一緒にパターンを作る素晴らしい仲間が2人もいます。チームがないメリさんに毎回嫉妬されていますが！ amirisuには英語と日本語の両方のパターンを同時に作るという他のメディアにはない高いハードルがあり、それをチームで必死にこなしています。リリースした後にいつも言い合う「今回もお疲れ様でした！」を聞くたび、1号の時と同じように涙が出そうになることはみんなには秘密です。

パターンはひとりでは作れないものです。次号からもたくさんの方の力を借りて、みんなでゴールまで走りたいと思っています。メリさん、10号、おめでとう！

Tokuko Ochiai

Casting Off...

Patterns

Errata is available at below url.
パターンのエラーはこちらに記載します.
http://www.amirisu.com/shop/errata/

Pattern Questions
Please go to Ravelry amirisu group and post your questions on a relevant thread.

本書に掲載するパターンのお問い合わせ
お問い合わせはRavelryのamirisuコミュニティボードよりお願いいたします。お電話でのお問い合わせではご回答できかねますので、その旨予めご了承ください。デザイナーと相談のうえ、ボード上で回答させていただきます。
http://www.ravelry.com/groups/amirisu

Keshi by Kirsten Johnstone

Specifications

Yarn

Sport weight yarn

(MC) Approximately 1045 (1110, 1175, 1310, 1450, 1595) yards / 955 (1015, 1075, 1200, 1330, 1460) m

Shibui Knits Linen (100% linen; 246 yards / 225m, 50g)

Sample shown in Clay 5 (5, 5, 6, 6, 7) skeins

Lace weight yarn

(CC) Approximately 555 (590, 625, 700, 770, 850) yards / 510 (540, 575, 640, 710, 780) m

Shibui Knits Silk Cloud (60% kid mohair / 40% silk; 330 yards / 300m, 25g)

Sample shown in Poppy 2 (2, 2, 3, 3, 3) skeins

Needles

A pair of US 4 (3.5 mm) straight needles

A US 4 (3.5 mm) 16" / 40 cm circular needle

or needle to obtain gauge

Gauge (after blocking)

24 sts & 30 rows = 4" / 10 cm in St st with US 4 (3.5 mm) needle and one strand each of MC and CC held together

24 sts & 30 rows = 4" / 10 cm in St st with US 4 (3.5 mm) needle and one strand of MC only

Sizes

Finished Chest Measurements: XS (S, M, L, XL, XXL) = 38½ (40½, 42½, 46½, 50½, 54½)" / 97 (102, 107, 117, 127, 137) cm

Ease: + 6½" / 16.5 cm

The sample was knit in size S with 5½" / 14 cm positive ease.

Tools

Stitch markers (2), tapestry needle, waste yarn, US E (3.5 mm) crochet hook, stitch holders

Skill Level

Stitch Guide

Folded hem detail

Remove waste yarn from Crochet provisional CO and place live sts on spare needle. Fold work on turning ridge so that spare needle is held in the left hand, behind main needle, purl sides of piece are facing each other and knit side is facing outward. Using right needle tip, *knit 1 st from main needle together with 1 st from spare needle; repeat from * to end.

I-Cord bind off

On left needle, use the Backward Loop Cast On to CO 3 sts. *K2, SSK, slip 3 sts from right needle to left; repeat from * until all but the 3 I-Cord sts have been bound off. Graft the beginning and the end of the I-Cord together.

Note

Top is worked in two pieces: Back and front, in St st.

Back is knitted flat, back and forth from the bottom up, in St st with 1 strand of MC.

Front is knitted flat, back and forth from the bottom up, in St st with 1 strand of MC and 1 strand of CC held together.

After back and front are worked, shoulders are grafted together. After blocking, sides are seamed from top of Folded hem to the underarm.

Top of armhole is then folded under shoulder to neck opening.

Neck is finished with I-Cord.

Instructions

Back

Using the crochet provisional cast on, waste yarn, and straight needles, CO 116 (122, 128, 140, 152, 164) sts. Join in one strand of MC.

Hem

Begin with a WS row, work in St st for 20 rows.

Knit 1 WS row (turning ridge).

Begin with a RS row, work in St st for 20 more rows.

Work Folded Hem Detail (see Stitch Guide).

Body

Begin with a WS row, work 26 rows or until work measures 6¼" / 16 cm from turning ridge in St st.

Shape back waist

Next row (WS): P 34 (36, 38, 42, 47, 51), PM, P48 (50, 52, 56, 58, 62), PM, P to end of row. 2 markers placed for Back darts.

Decrease row (RS): *K to 2 sts before M, K2tog, SM, SSK; repeat from * again, K to end. 4 sts decreased.

Work 7 rows even.

Repeat the last 8 rows 4 more times. 96 (102, 108, 120, 132, 144) sts.

Increase row (RS): *K to 1 st before M, M1R, K1, SM, K1, M1L; repeat from * again, K to end. 4 sts increased.

Work 7 rows even.

Repeat the last 8 rows 4 more times. 116 (122, 128, 140, 152, 164) sts.

Remove markers and work 4 rows even, ending with a WS row.

Work measures approx. 17½" / 44 cm from turning ridge.

Shape armhole

BO 2 sts at beg of next 2 rows. 112 (118, 124, 136, 148, 160) sts remain.

Work 52 (54, 56, 60, 64, 66) rows even, ending with a WS row.

Shape neck

Next row (RS): K 34 (36, 39, 44, 49, 54) and place on holder for right shoulder, BO 44 (46, 46, 48, 50, 52) sts, K to end. 34 (36, 39, 44, 49, 54) sts remain for left shoulder.

Shape left shoulder

Row 1 (WS): P.

Row 2: BO 3 sts, K to end.

Repeat the last 2 rows once more. 28 (30, 33, 38, 43, 48) sts remain.

Work 3 rows even.

Place sts on holder.

Shape right shoulder

Return 34 (36, 39, 44, 49, 54) held sts to needle and join one strand of MC with RS facing.

Row 1 (RS): K.

Row 2 (WS): BO 3 sts, P to end.

Repeat the last 2 rows once more. 28 (30, 33, 38, 43, 48) sts remain.

Work 3 rows even.

Place sts on holder.

Front

Using the crochet provisional cast on, waste yarn, and straight needles, CO 116 (122, 128, 140, 152, 164) sts. Join in one strand of MC and one strand of CC held together.

Hem

Begin with a WS row, work in St st for 20 rows.

Knit 1 WS row (turning ridge).

Begin with a RS row, work in St st for 20 more rows.

Work Folded Hem Detail (see Stitch Guide).

Body

Begin with a WS row, work 111 rows or until work measures 17½" / 44 cm from turning ridge in St st.

Shape armhole

BO 2 sts at beginning of next 2 rows. 112 (118, 124, 136, 148, 160) sts remain.

Work 52 (54, 56, 60, 64, 66) rows even, ending with a WS row.

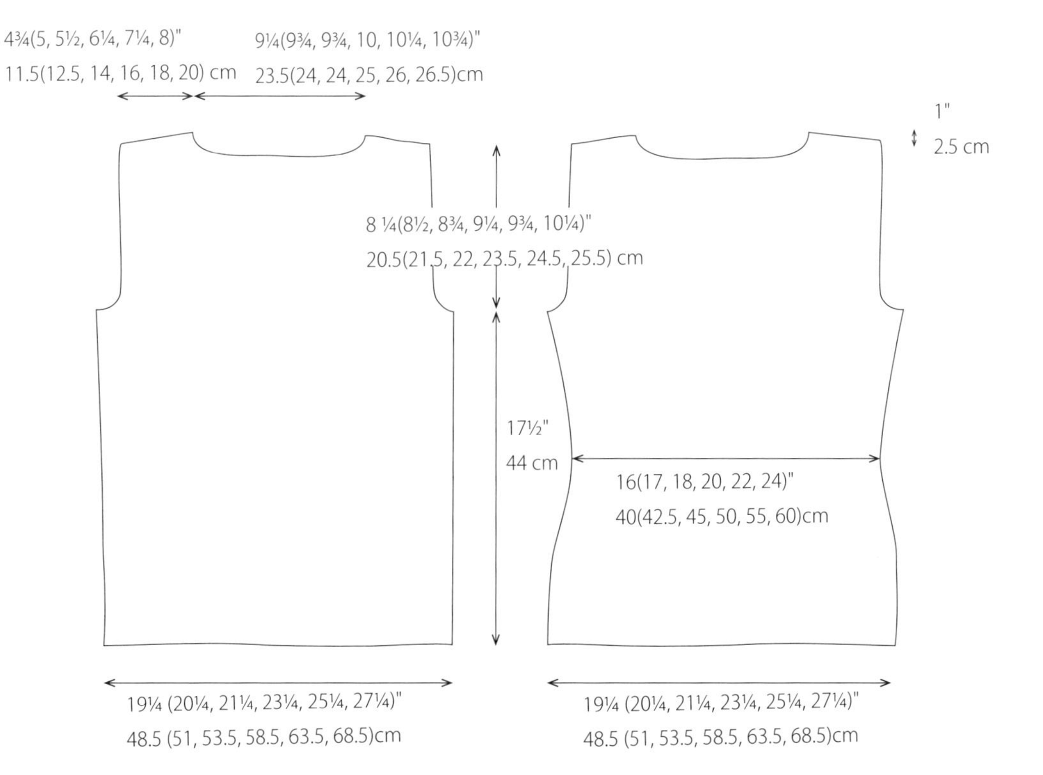

Shape neck

Next row (RS): K 34 (36, 39, 44, 49, 54) and place on holder for left shoulder, BO 44 (46, 46, 48, 50, 52) sts, K to end. 34 (36, 39, 44, 49, 54) sts remain for right shoulder.

Shape right shoulder

Row 1 (WS): P.

Row 2: BO 3 sts, K to end.

Repeat the last 2 rows once more. 28 (30, 33, 38, 43, 48) sts remain.

Work 3 rows even.

Place sts on holder.

Shape left shoulder

Return 34 (36, 39, 44, 49, 54) held sts to needle and join one strand of MC and one strand of CC with RS facing.

Row 1 (RS): K.

Row 2 (WS): BO 3 sts, P to end.

Repeat the last 2 rows once more. 28 (30, 33, 38, 43, 48) sts remain.

Work 3 rows even.

Using Kitchener stitch (see Stitch Guide), graft the Left front and Left back shoulder 28 (30, 33, 38, 43, 48) sts together. Repeat for Right front and Right back shoulder.

Finishing

Wash, dry, and block garment pieces gently following yarn manufacturer's instructions.

With WS together, use Mattress stitch to seam Front to Back at both sides with selvedges to RS, aligning pieces at top of Folded hem and underarm (do not seam Folded hem).

Separately, sew the open edges of the Folded hems closed (but do not seam Front to Back).

Weave in ends.

Neckband

With RS facing, fold top of each armhole under the shoulder and pin to inside neck edge. Using circular needle and one strand of MC, with RS facing and beginning at center back pick up and knit 128 (132, 132, 136, 140, 144) sts around neckline, picking up 6 sts through both the inside neck and top of armholes to secure each folded shoulder.

BO all sts using I-Cord bind off (see Stitch Guide).

TIP: Upon completion, we suggest placing the finished top on a dressform or coat hanger and steam block both shoulders, finger pressing the folded edge to give a neat and sharp finish.

詳細情報

Yarn

Sport Weight Yarn

(MC)約1045(1110, 1175, 1310, 1450, 1595) yards, 955(1015, 1075, 1200, 1330, 1460) m

Shibui Knits Linen (100% linen; 246 yards / 225 m, 50g)

サンプル色はClay 5(5, 5, 6, 6, 7)カセ

Lace Weight Yarn

(CC)約555 (590, 625, 700, 770, 850) yards, 510(540, 575, 640, 710, 780) m

Shibui Knits Silk Cloud (60% kid mohair / 40% silk; 330 yards / 300 m, 25g)

サンプル色はPoppy 2(2, 2, 3, 3, 3)カセ

Needles

1 x US 4 (3.5 mm)の2本針

1 x US 4 (3.5 mm) 16" / 40 cmの輪針

または, ゲージに合わせた太さの針

Gauge (ブロッキング後)

MCとCCの2本取りで, US4 (3.5 mm)の針を使用し, メリヤス編みで24目&30段 = 10 cm

MC1本取りで, US4 (3.5 mm)の針を使用し, メリヤス編みで24目&30段 = 10 cm

Sizes

出来上がり寸法: 胸囲XS(S, M, L, XL, XXL) = 97(102, 107, 117, 127, 137) cm

余裕: + 16.5 cm

モデルはSサイズを着用し, 余裕 として+14cm.

Tools

目数マーカー (2), 綴じ針, 別糸, US Eサイズ(3.5 mm)のかぎ針, ホルダー

Skill Level

Stitch Guide

Folded hem detail

別糸をはずしながら, かぎ針を用いた後でほどける作り目で作った目を, 予備の輪針に移す. 予備の輪針がメインの左針の後ろ側にくるように, 外表に折り返す. メインの針にある1目と予備の針にある1目を一緒に表編みで編む. これを最後まで繰り返す.

I-Cord bind off

左針に巻き増目で3目CO. *K2, SSK, 右針から左針へ3目すべり目. *からを最後まで繰り返す. 最後のIコード3目をBOし, 最初のIコードと最後のIコードをはぐ

Note

前後身頃に分けてメリヤス編みで編む. 後身頃はMC一本取りで, 往復編みでヘムから編む. 前身頃はMCとCCの2本取りで, 往復編みでヘムから編む.

前後身頃を編み終わった後で, 肩をはぎ合わせる. ブロッキングした後, ヘムの上端から脇下をはぎ合わせる. 最後に, 袖ぐりの上部を内側に折り返し, 拾い目をした襟ぐりと一緒に, I-Cordで伏せる.

編みかた

後身頃

別糸を使用し, かぎ針を用いた後でほどける作り目でCO 116 (122, 128, 140, 152, 164)目.

MCを1取りで編み始める.

ヘム

WSから編み始め, メリヤス編みで20段.

次のWS段を全てK. (ヘムの折り返し部分)

RS段から, メリヤス編みで20段.

ステッチガイドを参照に, 折り返してヘムを作る.

身頃

WS段から編み始め, メリヤス編みで26段もしくは折り返し線から16cmになるまで編む.

後ろ身頃のウエストシェイピング

次の段(WS): P34(36, 38, 42, 47, 51), PM, P48(50, 52, 56, 58, 62), PM, 最後までP. 2つのマーカーはバックダーツ位置を示す.

減目段(RS): *Mの2目前までK, K2tog, SM, SSK; *からをもう一度繰り返す, 最後までK. 4目減目.

7段メリヤス編み.

上記の8段をさらに4回繰り返す. 計96 (102, 108, 120, 132, 144)目.

増目段(RS): *Mの1目前までK, M1R, K1, SM, K1, M1L; *からをもう一度繰り返す, 最後までK. 4目増目.

7段メリヤス編み.

上記の8段をさらに4回繰り返す. 計116 (122, 128, 140, 152, 164)目.

マーカーを外し, 4段メリヤス編みし, WSで編み終わる. 折り返し線から44cm.

袖ぐりシェイピング

次の段(RS): BO2目, 最後までK.

次の段(WS): BO2目, 最後までP. 計112 (118, 124, 136, 148, 160)目.

52 (54, 56, 60, 64, 66)段メリヤス編みし, WSで編み終わる.

襟ぐりシェイピング

次の段(RS): K34 (36, 39, 44, 49, 54), これを右肩の目としてホルダーに目を休める, BO44 (46, 46, 48, 50, 52)目, 最後までK. 残り34 (36, 39, 44, 49, 54)目が左肩の目になる.

左肩シェイピング

段1(WS): 全てP.

段2: BO3目, 最後までK.

最後の2段をさらに1回繰り返す. 計28 (30, 33, 38, 43, 48)目.

3段メリヤス編み.

ホルダーに目を休める.

右肩シェイピング

ホルダーに休めた34 (36, 39, 44, 49, 54)目を編み針に移しMCを1本取りでRSから編み始める.

段1(RS): 全てK.

段2 (WS): BO3目, 最後までP.

最後の2段をさらに1回繰り返す. 計28 (30, 33, 38, 43, 48)目.

3段メリヤス編み.

ホルダーに目を休める.

前身頃

別糸を使用し, かぎ針を用いた後でほどける作り目でCO 116 (122, 128, 140, 152, 164)目. MCとCCを2本取りで編む.

ヘム

WSから編み始め, メリヤス編みで20段.

次のWS段を全てK. (ヘムの折り返し部分)

RS段から, メリヤス編みで20段.

ステッチガイドを参照に, 折り返してヘムを作る.

身頃

WSから編み始め, メリヤスで111段, もしくは折り返し線から44cmになるまで編む.

袖ぐりシェイピング

次の段(RS): BO2目, 最後までK.

次の段(WS): BO2目, 最後までP. 計112 (118, 124, 136, 148, 160)目.

52 (54, 56, 60, 64, 66)段メリヤス編みし, WSで編み終わる.

襟ぐりシェイピング

次の段(RS): K34 (36, 39, 44, 49, 54), これを左肩の目としてホルダーに目を休める, BO44 (46, 46, 48, 50, 52)目, 最後までK. 残りの34 (36, 39, 44, 49, 54)目が右肩の目になる.

右肩シェイピング

段1(WS): 全てP.

段2: BO3目, 最後までK.

最後の2段をさらに1回繰り返す. 計28 (30, 33, 38, 43, 48)目.

3段メリヤス編み.

ホルダーに目を休める.

左肩シェイピング

ホルダーに休めた34 (36, 39, 44, 49, 54)目を編み針に移しMCとCCを2本取りでRSから編み始める.

段1(RS): 全てK.

段2(WS): BO3目, 最後までP.

最後の2段をさらに1回繰り返す. 計28 (30, 33, 38, 43, 48)目.

3段メリヤス編み.

前後身頃の左肩28 (30, 33, 38, 43, 48)目をメリヤスはぎではぎあわせる. 右肩も同様にはぎあわせる.

仕上げ

用いた糸の説明書に従い洗い, ブロッキングする. WSを内側にして, ヘムの上端と袖下を合わせて, 前後身頃のRSの端目をすくい綴じではぎ合わせる. (ヘム部分は, はぎ合わせない.)

別に, ヘムのはぎ合わせていない端目を綴じる.

糸始末をする.

襟ぐり

RSを見ながら, 両肩の袖ぐり上部を内側に折り返してピンで固定する.

輪針を使用し, MCの1本取りで, 襟ぐりの後身頃中心から始めて128 (132, 132, 136, 140, 144)目を拾い目する. その際に内側に折り返した袖ぐりの目と襟ぐりの目を6目は一緒に拾い編む.

I-Code bind offで, 全てBO. 仕上げとして, 編みあがったトップスをマネキンかハンガーにかけて肩の折り返し部分を指で整え, スチームブロックする.

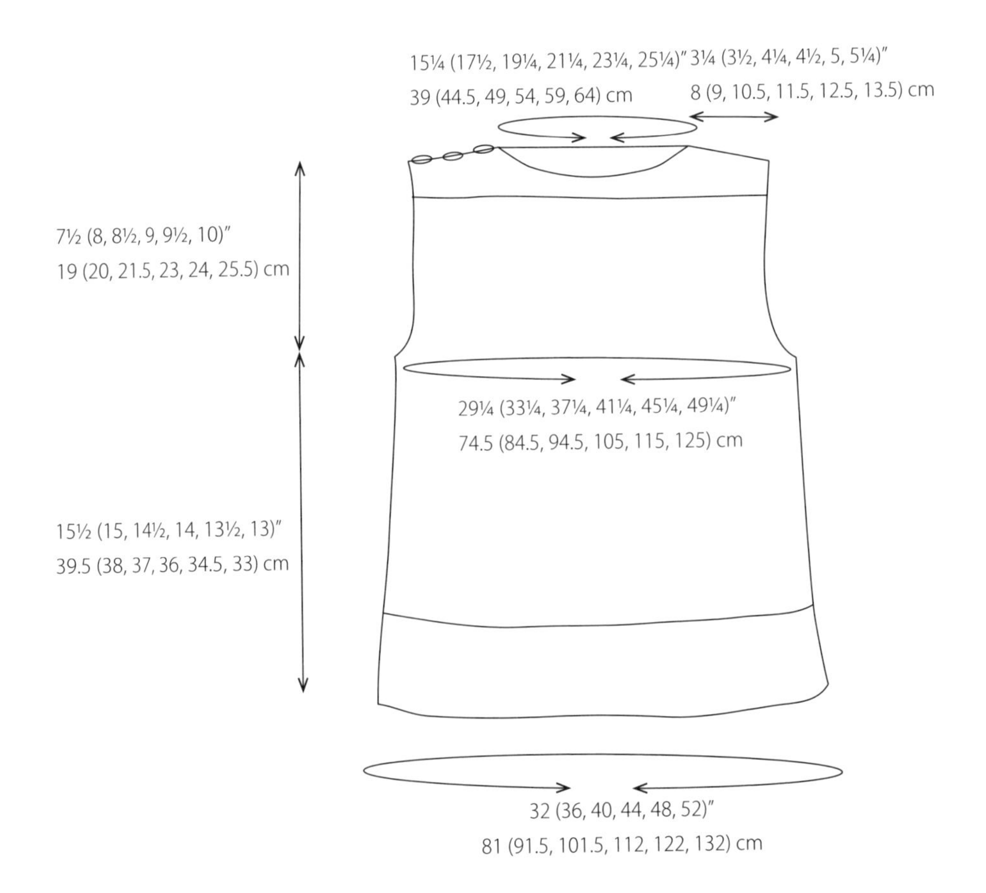

Sango by Melissa LaBarre

Specifications

Yarn

Sport weight yarn

Approximately 600 (700, 800, 900, 1000, 1100) yards, 550 (640, 730, 825, 915, 1005) m

4 (5, 5, 6, 7, 7) skeins of Quince and Co. Willet (100% Cleaner Cotton; 160 yards / 146 m, 50g)

Sample is shown in Oar

Needle

A US 5 (3.75 mm) 24" / 60 cm circular needle

Gauge (after blocking)

24 sts & 32 rows = 4" / 10 cm in St st with US 5 (3.75 mm) needle

Sizes

Finished chest measurements : XS (S, M, L, XL, XXL) = 29 ¼ (33¼ , 37¼ , 41¼ , 45¼ , 49¼)" /75 (85, 95, 105, 115, 125) cm

Ease: -1" / -2.5 cm

The sample was knit in size S with -½" / -1cm negative ease.

Tools

Stitch markers (2), tapestry needle, waste yarn, ½" / 1.25 cm buttons (3)

Skill Level

Note

This piece is knit in the round, from the bottom up, to the armholes. Half of stitches are then placed on waste yarn and front and back are worked back and forth separately for the rest of the piece.

Instructions

Body

Bottom Hem

Using long-tail method, CO 96 (108, 120, 132, 144, 156) sts, PM, CO 96 (108, 120, 132, 144, 156) sts. Total 192 (216, 240, 264, 288, 312) sts.

PM for beginning of round and join in the round, being careful not to twist.

Begin working from Zig Zag Lace chart.

Work rounds 1-15 2 times total.

Next round : P all sts.

Next round : K all sts.

Next round : P all sts.

Side Shaping

Decrease round 1: K to 2 sts before end of round, SSK, SM. (1 st decreased)

Decrease round 2: K2tog, K to 2 sts before M, SSK, SM, K2tog, K to end of round, SM. (3 sts decreased) 188 (212, 236, 260, 284, 308) sts.

Repeat these 2 decrease rounds, every 11th and 12th round for 6 times total.

168 (192, 216, 240, 264, 288) sts.

Work in St st for 2" / 5 cm.

Increase round 1: K to 1 st before end of round, M1R, K1, SM. (1 st increased)

Increase round 2: K1, M1L, K to 1 st before M, M1R, K1, SM, K1, M1L, K to end of round, SM. (3 sts increased) 172 (196, 220, 244, 268, 292) sts.

Work in St st until piece measures 15.5 (15, 14.5, 14, 13.5, 13)" / 39.5 (38, 37, 35.5, 34, 33) cm from CO edge.

Separate front and back

Remove BOR marker. Move next 86 (98, 110, 122, 134, 146) sts to waste yarn.

Back

Work back and forth in St st until back measures 6.5 (7, 7.5, 8, 8.5, 9)" / 16.5 (18, 19, 20, 21.5, 23) cm. End after a WS row.

Shape Back Neck

K29 (32, 35, 38, 41, 44), attach new ball of yarn and BO 28 (34, 40, 46, 52, 58) sts. K to end of row.

Next row (WS): P29 (32, 35, 38, 41, 44) across 1st shoulder, BO 6 sts across next shoulder, P to end of row.

Next row (RS): K across 1st shoulder. BO 6 sts across next shoulder K to end.

Next row (WS): BO 8 sts, P to end of shoulder. P across

2nd shoulder.

Next row (RS): BO 8 sts, K to end. K across 2nd shoulder.

Next row (WS): 15 (18, 21, 24, 27, 30) sts remain.

BO remaining sts on each shoulder. Break yarn.

With RS facing, pick up and knit1 st for every st 86 (98, 110, 122, 134, 146) sts across top edge. Work back and forth in St st for 8 rows, ending after a RS row.

BO all sts in purl.

Front

Attach yarn on RS and work back and forth in St st until back measures 6.5 (7, 7.5, 8, 8.5, 9)" / 16.5 (18, 19, 20, 21.5, 23) cm. End after a WS row.

Shape Front Neck

K33 (36, 39, 42, 45, 48), attach new ball of yarn and BO 20 (26, 32, 38, 44, 50) sts. K to end of row.

Next row (WS): P33 (36, 39, 42, 45, 48) across 1st shoulder, BO 6 sts across next shoulder, P to end of row.

Next row (RS): K across 1st shoulder. BO 6 sts across next shoulder K to end.

Next row (WS): P27 (30, 33, 36, 39, 42) across 1st shoulder, BO 4 sts across next shoulder, P to end of row.

Next row (RS): K across 1st shoulder. BO 4 sts across next shoulder K to end.

Next row (WS): BO 8 sts, P to end of shoulder. P across 2nd shoulder.

Next row (RS): BO 8 sts, K to end. K across 2nd shoulder.

Next row (WS): 15 (18, 21, 24, 27, 30) sts remain.

BO remaining sts on each shoulder. Break yarn.

With RS facing, pick up and knit1 st for every st 86 (98, 110, 122, 134, 146) sts across top edge. Work back and forth in St st for 8 rows, ending after a RS row.

Next row (WS): K22 (24, 27, 30, 33, 34), BO remaining sts. Break yarn.

Buttonhole row (RS): Join yarn and make buttonholes as follow.

K1 (2, 2, 3, 3, 4), K2tog, YO, K6 (7, 8, 9, 10, 11), K2tog, YO, K6 (6, 7, 8, 9, 10), K2tog, YO, K3 (3, 4, 4, 5, 5).

Next Row (WS): P all sts.

BO all sts in purl.

Seam right shoulder.

Armhole Finishing

Pick up and knit 3 sts for every 4 rows around armhole. Do not join. BO in purl on WS. Repeat for next armhole.

Finishing

Weave in ends. Block using water or steam. Sew buttons opposite buttonholes on left shoulder.

詳細情報

Yarn

Sport weight yarn

約600 (700, 800, 900, 1000, 1100) yards, 550 (640, 730, 825, 915, 1005) m

Quince and Co. Willet (100% Cleaner Cotton; 160 yards / 146 m, 50g) 4 (5, 5, 6, 7, 7) かせ

サンプル色は Oar

Needle

1 x US 5 (3.75 mm) 24" / 60 cmの輪針

Gauge (ブロッキング後)

US 5 (3.75 mm) を使用し, メリヤス編みで24目 & 32段= 10 cm

Sizes

出来上がり寸法 : 胸囲XS (S, M, L, XL, XXL) = 75 (85, 95, 105, 115, 125) cm

Ease: -2.5 cm

モデルはSサイズを着用し, 余裕 として-1cm.

Tools

目数M (2), とじ針, 別糸, ボタン1.25 cm (3)

Skill Level

Note

ボトムから輪にして身頃を編み, 脇下で前後を分ける.以降, 往復編みで各身頃を仕上げる.

編みかた

身頃

ヘム

指で掛ける作り目でCO 96 (108, 120, 132, 144, 156)目, PM, CO 96 (108, 120, 132, 144, 156) 目. 計192 (216, 240, 264, 288, 312)目.

編み始めのMを入れ, ねじらないように気をつけながら, 輪にする.

1-15周のZig Zag Laceをチャートを参照に, 計2回編む.

次の周: 全てP.

次の周: 全てK.

次の周: 全てP.

サイドシェイピング

減目周 1: 最後の2目前までK, SSK, SM. (1目減目)

減目周 2: K2tog, Mの2目前までK , SSK, SM, K2tog, 最後までK, SM. (3目減目)　計188 (212, 236, 260, 284, 308)目.

減目周1&2を, 11&12周毎に, 計6回繰り返す.

計168 (192, 216, 240, 264, 288)目.

メリヤス編みで, 5 cm編む.

増目周 1: 最後の1目前までK, M1R, K1, SM. (1目増目)

増目周 2: K1, M1L, Mの1目前までK, M1R, K1, SM, K1, M1L, 最後までK, SM. (3目 増目)　計172 (196, 220, 244, 268, 292)目.

メリヤス編みで, 作り目から 39.5(38, 37, 35.5, 34, 33) cmになるまで編む.

前後身頃をわける

編み始めのMを外し, 次の86 (98, 110, 122, 134, 146)目を別糸に休ませる.

後ろ身頃

メリヤス編みで, 後ろ身頃が16.5 (18, 19, 20, 21.5, 23) cmになるまで編む. WS段で終わる.

シェイピング

Note: ここからもう一つ新しい糸工をつけ, 両肩いっぺんに編んでいく.

K29 (32, 35, 38, 41, 44), 新しい糸をつけてBO 28 (34, 40, 46, 52, 58) 目.最後までK.

次の段(WS): 1つ目の肩としてP29 (32, 35, 38, 41, 44).次の肩からBO 6目, 最後までP.

次の段(RS): 1つ目の肩を全てK.次の肩からBO 6目, 最後までK.

次の段(WS): BO 8目, 1つ目の肩を全てP. 次の肩も全てP.

次の段(RS): BO 8目, 1つ目の肩を全てK. 次の肩も全てK.

次の段(WS): 各肩15 (18, 21, 24, 27, 30)目を全てBO. 糸を切る.

RSを見ながら, 後ろ身頃トップエッジ全ての目から1目ずつ, 86 (98, 110, 122, 134, 146)目になるように拾う. メリヤス編みで8段編み, RS段で終わる.

全てPを編むようにBO.

前身頃

RSを見ながら糸をつけ, メリヤス編みで, 前身頃が16.5 (18, 19, 20, 21.5, 23) cmになるまで編む. WS段で終わる.

シェイピング

Note: ここからもう一つ新しい糸玉をつけ, 両肩いっぺんに編んでいく.

K33 (36, 39, 42, 45, 48), 新しい糸をつけてBO 20 (26, 32, 38, 44, 50) 目.最後までK.

次の段(WS): 1つ目の肩としてP33(36, 39, 42, 45, 48).次の肩からBO 6目, 最後までP.

次の段(RS): 1つ目の肩を全てK.次の肩からBO 6目, 最後までK.

次の段(WS): 1つ目の肩としてP27 (30, 33, 36, 39, 42).次の肩からBO 4目, 最後までP.

次の段(RS): 1つ目の肩を全てK.次の肩からBO 4目, 最後までK.

次の段(WS): BO8, 1つ目の肩を全てP.次の肩も全てP.

次の段(RS): BO8, 1つ目の肩を全てK. 次の肩も全てK.

次の段(WS): 各肩15 (18, 21, 24, 27, 30)目を全てBO.糸を切る.

RSを見ながら, 前身頃トップエッジ全ての目から1目ずつ, 86 (98, 110, 122, 134, 146)目になるように拾う. メリヤス編みで8段編み, RS段で終わる.

次の段(WS): K22 (24, 27, 30, 33, 34), 残り全ての目をBO.糸を切る.

ボタンホール段(RS):　新たに糸をつけてボタンホールを次のように編む.

K1 (2, 2, 3, 3, 4), K2tog, YO, K6 (7, 8, 9, 10, 11), K2tog, YO, K6 (6, 7, 8, 9, 10), K2tog, YO, K3 (3, 4, 4, 5, 5).

次の段(WS): 全てP.

全てPを編むようにBO.

右肩を綴じる.

袖ぐりの仕上げ

袖ぐりの周りを, 4段に3目の間隔で目を拾う. 輪にせず編み地を返し, 全てPを編むようにBO.

仕上げ

糸始末をし, ブロッキングまたはスチームを当てる.

左肩にボタンを縫い付ける.

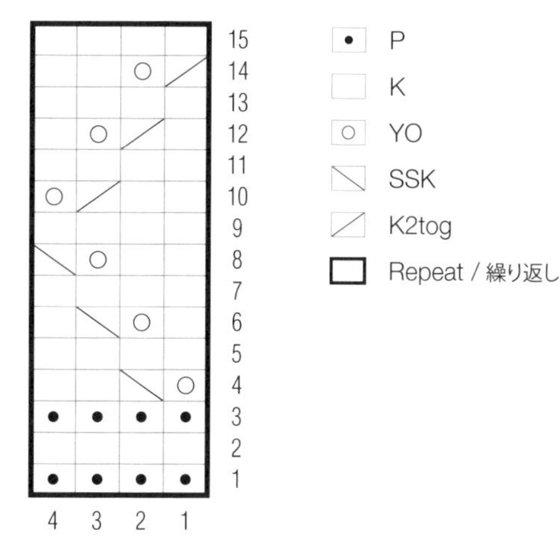

Asagi by Bristol Ivy

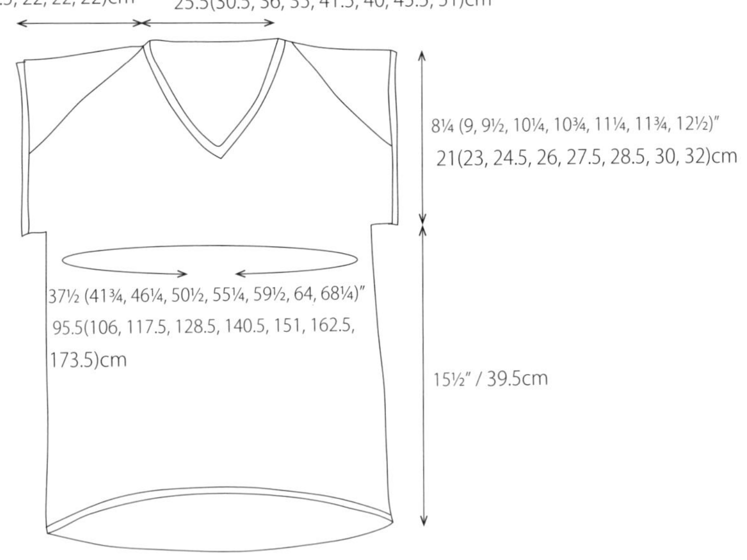

Specifications

Yarn

Light fingering weight yarn

Approx. 805 (945, 1055, 1195, 1330, 1455, 1575, 1680) yards, 740 (865, 965, 1095, 1220, 1335, 1445, 1540) m

2 (2, 3, 3, 3, 3, 4, 4) skeins of Jill Draper Makes Stuff Esopus (100% US grown Superwash Merino wool; 500 yards / 457 m, 113g)

Sample shown in Celadon

Needles

A US 4 (3.5 mm) 32" circular needle

A US 3 (3.25 mm) 32" circular needle

A US 3 (3.25 mm) 16" circular needle

A set of US 3 (3.25 mm) DPNs

or needle to obtain gauge

Gauge (after blocking)

24.5 sts & 41 rows / rounds = 4" / 10 cm in St st with US 4 (3.5 mm) needle

Sizes

Finished Bust Measurements: XS (S, M, L, XL, 2XL, 3XL, 4XL) = 37½ (41¾, 46¼, 50½, 55¼, 59½, 64, 68¼)" / 95.5 (106, 117.5, 128.5, 140.5, 151, 162.5, 173.5) cm

Ease: + 6 - 8" / + 15 - 20.5 cm

The sample was knit in size S with 7" / 18 cm positive ease.

Tools

Stitch markers (2), tapestry needle, waste yarn

Skill Level

Note

Tank is worked from the top down; back is worked as for a traditional raglan; sleeves are worked in lace pattern with raglan increases incorporated into it. Once lace pattern is complete, sleeve sts are bound off and the back is continued down to the underarm, then place on holder. Front sts are picked up in selvedge along sleeves and worked out and down to underarm, with increases worked at neck and armhole edge. At armhole, fronts are joined with a CO in the center front, and then joined with the back to work in the round to hem in St st. Hem, neck, and sleeves are finished with 1x1 ribbing.

Set up chart

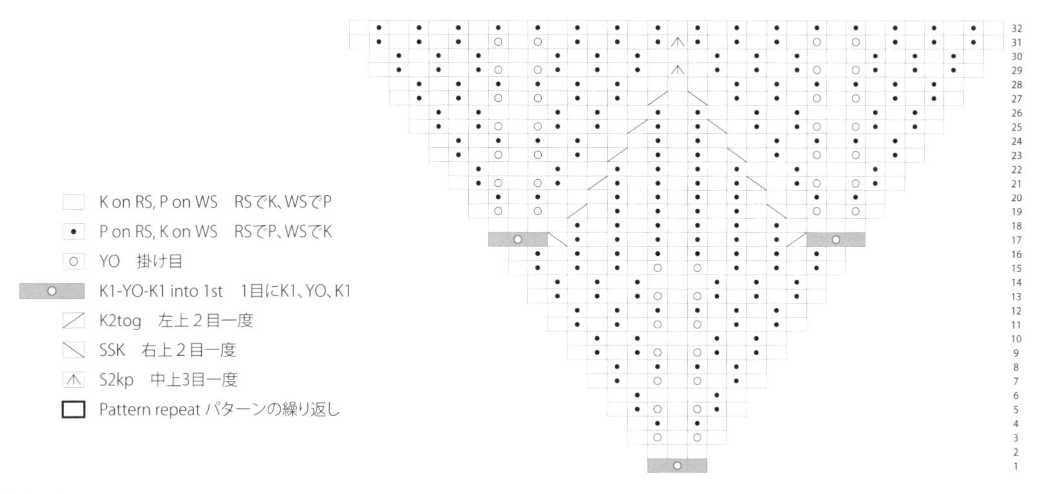

Main chart

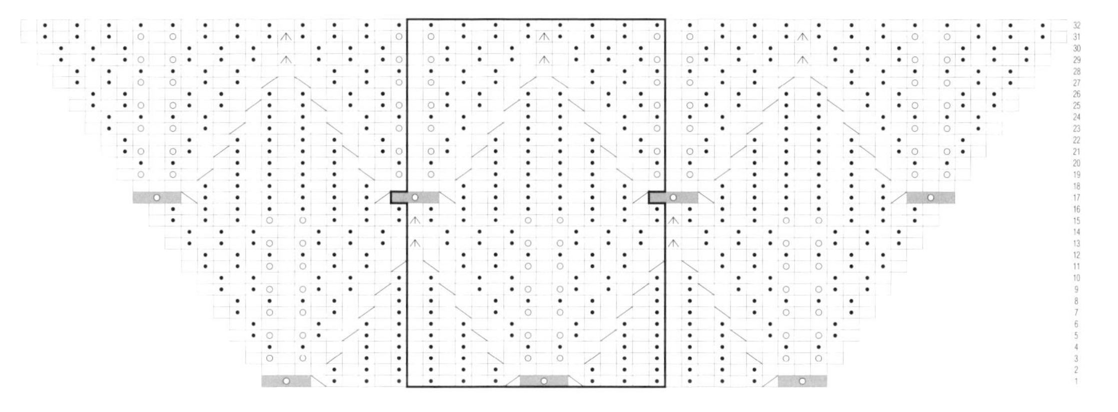

Instructions

Yoke

With long-tail cast on, CO 71 (84, 98, 95, 109, 106, 120, 133) sts using larger circular needle. Do not join.

Next row (WS): P2, PM, P to last 2 sts, PM, P2.

Next row (RS): K1, work row 1 of Set-up chart to M, SM, K1, M1L, K to 1 st before M, M1R, K1, SM, work row 1 of Set-up chart to last st, K1. 6 sts increased.

Next row: P1, work row 2 of Set-up chart to m, SM, P to M, SM, work row 2 of Set-up chart to last st, P1.

Rep previous two rows, continuing through row 32 of Set-up chart. 90 sts increased.

167 (180, 194, 191, 205, 202, 216, 229) sts.

Next row (RS): K1, work row 1 of Main chart to M, SM, K1, M1L, K to 1 st before M, M1R, K1, SM, work row 1 of Main chart to last st, K1. 6 sts increased.

Next row: P1, work row 2 of Main chart to M, SM, P to M, SM, work row 2 of Main chart to last st, P1.

Rep these two rows, continuing through row 16 (16, 16, 32, 32, 32, 32, 32) of Main chart. 42 (42, 42, 90, 90, 90, 90, 90) sts increased. 215 (228, 242, 287, 301, 298, 312, 325) sts.

Sizes - (- , - ,- , - , 2XL, 3XL, 4XL) only:

Rep rows 1-16 of Main chart once more, working bracketed repeat 3 times. - (- , - , - , - , 48, 48, 48) sts increased. - (- , - , - , - , 346, 360, 373) sts.

All sizes resume:

215 (228, 242, 287, 301, 346, 360, 373) sts on needle.

Next row (RS): BO next 50 (50, 50, 66, 66, 82, 82, 82) sts knitwise loosely to M, RM, K to M, RM, BO next 50 (50, 50, 66, 66, 82, 82, 82) sts knitwise loosely to end. 115 (128, 142, 155, 169, 182, 196, 209) sts on needle. Break yarn.

Back Yoke

Next row (WS): Rejoin yarn reading to work a WS row on remaining sts. Purl.

Work even in St st until yoke measures 3¾ (4¼, 4¾, 4¼, 4¾, 4, 4½, 5)" / 9.5 (11, 12, 11, 12, 10.5, 11.5, 13) cm from BO beginning of back yoke. Place all sts on holder, break yarn, and set aside.

Left Front Yoke

Fabric facing RS, in left side of yoke from neck edge and with larger needle, pick up and knit 32 (32, 32, 43, 43, 53, 53, 53) sts at a rate of approx 2 sts every 3 rows. Do not join.

Next row (WS): Purl.

Next row (RS): K1, M1L, K to last st, M1R, K1. 2 sts increased.

Next row: Purl.

Next row: K to last st, M1R, K1.

Rep these 4 rows 7 (9, 10, 9, 10, 8, 9, 11) more times. 56 (62, 65, 73, 76, 80, 83, 89) sts.

Place all sts on holder, break yarn, and set aside.

Right Front Yoke

Fabric facing RS, in right side of yoke from sleeve edge and with larger needle, pick up and knit 32 (32, 32, 43, 43, 53, 53, 53) sts. Do not join.

Next row (WS): Purl.

Next row (RS): K1, M1L, K to last st, M1R, K1. 2 sts increased.

Next row: Purl.

Next row: K1, M1L, K to end.

Rep these 4 rows 7 (9, 10, 9, 10, 8, 9, 11) more times. 56 (62, 65, 73, 76, 80, 83, 89) sts.

Next row (WS): Purl.

Do not break yarn.

Body

With working yarn, K56 (62, 65, 73, 76, 80, 83, 89) right front yoke sts, then, using cable cast on, CO 3 (4, 12, 9, 17, 22, 30, 31) sts, then K56 (62, 65, 73, 76, 80, 83, 89) held left front yoke sts, then K115 (128, 142, 155, 169, 182, 196, 209) held back yoke sts. PM for BOR and join to work in the round, being careful not to twist. 230 (256, 284, 310, 338, 364, 392, 418) sts on needle.

Work even in St st in the round until piece measures 14½" / 37 cm from join.

Ribbing

With smaller, longer circular needle, *K1, P1, repeat from * to end of round. Work in 1x1 rib as established for 1" / 2.5 cm. BO all sts knitwise loosely with larger needle.

Neckband

Starting at the right shoulder and with smaller, shorter circular needle, pick up and knit 69 (82, 96, 93, 107, 104, 118, 131) sts in original CO at a rate of 1 st per st, then pick up and knit 21 (27, 29, 27, 29, 24, 27, 32) sts in Left Front Yoke rows at a rate of approx 2 sts every 3 rows, then pick up and knit 3 (4, 12, 9, 17, 22, 30, 31) sts in center front CO sts at a rate of 1 st per st, then pick up and knit 21 (27, 29, 27, 29, 24, 27, 32) sts in Right Front Yoke rows at a rate of approx 2 sts every 3 rows. Join to work in the round and PM for BOR. 114 (140, 166, 156, 182, 174, 202, 226) sts.

*K1, P1, repeat from * to end of round. Work in 1x1 rib as established in 1x1 rib for ½" / 1.5 cm. BO all sts knitwise loosely with larger needle.

Armhole Edging

Starting at the bottom of the right underarm and with DPNs, pick up and knit 21 (27, 29, 27, 29, 24, 27, 32) sts in right back to BO at a rate of 2 sts every 3 rows, then pick up and knit 49 (49, 49, 65, 65, 81, 81, 81) sts in BO at a rate of 1 st every st, and 22 (28, 30, 28, 30, 25, 28, 33) sts in right front to end at a rate of 2 sts every 3 rows. Join to work in the rnd and PM for BOR. 92 (104, 108, 120, 124, 130, 136, 146) sts.

K1, P1, repeat from * to end of round. Work in 1x1 rib as established in 1x1 rib for ½" / 1.5 cm. BO all sts knitwise loosely with larger needle.

Repeat for second armhole edging, picking up first in left front then in left back.

Finishing

Weave in all ends and block to measurements.

詳細情報

Yarn

Light fingering weight yarn

約805 (945, 1055, 1195, 1330, 1455, 1575, 1680) yards, 740 (865, 965, 1095, 1220, 1335, 1445, 1540) m

Jill Draper Makes Stuff Esopus (100% US grown Superwash Merino wool; 500 yards / 457 m, 113g) 2 (2, 3, 3, 3, 3, 4, 4) カセ

サンプル色は Celadon

Needles

1 x US 4 (3.5mm) 32" / 80cmの輪針

1 x US 3 (3.25mm) 32" / 80cmの輪針

1 x US 3 (3.25mm) 16" / 40cmの輪針

1 x US 3 (3.25mm) の4本針

またはゲージに合わせた太さの針

Gauge (ブロッキング後)

US4 (3.5mm)の針を使用し, メリヤス編みで24.5目 & 41 段/周 = 10cm

Sizes

出来上がり寸法 : XS (S, M, L, XL, 2XL, 3XL, 4XL) = 95.5 (106, 117.5, 128.5, 140.5, 151, 162.5, 173.5) cm

余裕 : +15 - 20.5cm

モデルはSサイズを着用し, 余裕 として+18 cm.

Tools

目数マーカー (2), 綴じ針, 別糸

Skill Level

Note

トップダウンのタンクトップ.後ろ身頃をトラディショナルなラグランシェープで, 袖はラグランの増目が組み込まれているレース模様で編む.レース模様を編み終えたら袖の目を伏せ, 後ろ身頃を引き続き脇下まで往復編みし, 別糸に休ませる. 前身頃は袖(レース模様)の端目から目を拾い, 増目をしながら脇下まで往復編みで編む.脇下で前中心のCOを入れながら左右の前身頃をつなぎ, それから後ろ身頃をつないで, 輪にして裾までメリヤス編みで編む.裾, 襟ぐり, 袖口は1目ゴム編みで仕上げる.

編みかた

ヨーク

大きい方の輪針を使い, Long tail cast onでCO 71 (84, 98, 95, 109, 106, 120, 133)目.輪にしない.

次の段(WS): P2, PM, 最後の2 目前までP, PM, P2.

次の段(RS): K1, Set-up chartの段1をMまで編む, SM, K1, M1L, Mの1目前までK , M1R, K1, SM, Set-up chartの段1を最後の1目前まで編む, K1.6 目増目.

次の段: P1, Set-up chartの段2をMまで編む, SM, MまでP, SM, Set-up chartの段2を最後の1目前まで編む , P1.

最後の2段をSet-up chart の段32を編み終えるまで繰り返す.90目増目.

167 (180, 194, 191, 205, 202, 216, 229)目.

次 の 段(RS): K1, Main chartの 段1をMま で 編 む, SM, K1, M1L, Mの1目前までK, M1R, K1, SM, Main chartの段1を最後の1目前まで編む, K1.6目増目.

次の段: P1, Main chartの段2をMまで編む, SM, MまでP, SM, Main chartの段2を最後の1目前まで編む, P1.

最後の2段を, Main chart の 段16 (16, 16, 32, 32, 32, 32, 32)を編むまで繰り返す.42 (42, 42, 90, 90, 90, 90, 90) 目増目.計215 (228, 242, 287, 301, 298, 312, 325) 目.

- (-, -, -, -, 2XL, 3XL, 4XL)サイズのみ:

Main chartの段1-16を, もう一度繰り返す(1段につき, 太枠部分は3回繰り返す). - (-, -, -, -, 48, 48, 48) 目増目.

計 - (-, -, -, -, 346, 360, 373) 目.

全てのサイズ:

計215 (228, 242, 287, 301, 346, 360, 373)目.

次の段(RS): 次のMまで50 (50, 50, 66, 66, 82, 82, 82)目を, Kを編むように針を入れ緩めにBO, RM, MまでK, RM, 最後の50 (50, 50, 66, 66, 82, 82, 82)目をKを編むように針を入れゆったりとBO.計115 (128, 142, 155, 169, 182, 196, 209)目.糸を切る.

後ろヨーク

次の段(WS): WSから開始, 針に残っている目を全てP.

メリヤス編みで, 後ろヨークがBOから 9.5 (11, 12, 11, 12, 10.5, 11.5, 13) cmになるまで編む. 糸を切り, 全ての目を別糸に休ませる.

左前ヨーク

大きい方の針を使用しRSを見ながら, 左前ヨークの目を首側から3段につき2 目の間隔で32 (32, 32, 43, 43, 53, 53, 53)目拾う.輪にしない.

次の段(WS): 全てP.

次の段(RS): K1, M1L, 最後の1目前までK, M1R, K1.2目増目.

次の段: 全てP.

次の段: 最後の1目前までK, M1R, K1.

最後の4段をあと 7 (9, 10, 9, 10, 8, 9, 11)回繰り返す.計56 (62, 65, 73, 76, 80, 83, 89)目.

糸を切り, 全ての目を別糸に休ませる.

右前ヨーク

大きい方の針を使用しRSを見ながら, 右前ヨークの目を袖側から, 32 (32, 32, 43, 43, 53, 53, 53)目拾う.輪にしない.

次の段(WS): 全てP.

次の段(RS): K1, M1L, 最後の1目前までK, M1R, K1.2 目増目.

次の段: 全てP.

次の段: K1, M1L, 最後までK.

最後の4段をあと 7 (9, 10, 9, 10, 8, 9, 11)回繰り返す.計56 (62, 65, 73, 76, 80, 83, 89)目.

次の段(WS): 全てP.

糸は切らない.

身頃

引き続き, 右前ヨークからK56 (62, 65, 73, 76, 80, 83, 89)目, cable cast onで, CO 3 (4, 12, 9, 17, 22, 30, 31) 目, 別糸に休めておいた左前ヨークからK56 (62, 65, 73, 76, 80, 83, 89)目, 別糸に休めておいた後ろヨークからK115 (128, 142, 155, 169, 182, 196, 209)目. 編み始めのマーカーをつけて, ねじらないように注意しながら輪にする.計230 (256, 284, 310, 338, 364, 392, 418)目.

メリヤス編みで, 身頃を輪にしたところから 37 cmになるまで編む.

裾

小さい方の針(80 cm)を使用し， 1目ゴム編みを2.5 cm編む.大きい方の針を使って, Kを編むように針を入れゆったりとBO.

首回り

小さい方の針(40 cm)を使用し, 右肩からスタートして次の通り拾い目をする.

最初のCOから1目につき1目の間隔で69 (82, 96, 93, 107, 104, 118, 131) 目, 左前ヨークから3段につき2 目の間隔で 21 (27, 29, 27, 29, 24, 27, 32) 目, 中心のCOから1目につき1目の間隔で 3 (4, 12, 9, 17, 22, 30, 31)目, 右前ヨークから3段につき2 目の間隔で 21 (27, 29, 27, 29, 24, 27, 32) 目.編み始めのマーカーをつけて, ねじらないように注意しながら輪にする.計114 (140, 166, 156, 182, 174, 202, 226) 目.

1目ゴム編みを1.5 cm編む.大きい方の針を使って, Kを編むように針を入れゆったりとBO.

袖回り

4本針を使用し, 右袖の脇下からスタートして次の通り目を拾う.

後ろ身頃のBOから3段につき2 目の間隔で21 (27, 29, 27, 29, 24, 27, 32)目, レース模様のBOから1目につき1目の間隔で49 (49, 49, 65, 65, 81, 81, 81)目, 前身頃のBOから3段につき2 目の間隔で22 (28, 30, 28, 30, 25, 28, 33)目拾う.編み始めのマーカーをつけて輪にする.計92 (104, 108, 120, 124, 130, 136, 146)目.

1目ゴム編みを1.5 cm編む.大きい方の針を使って, Kを編むように針を入れゆったりとBO.

左袖も, 右袖と同様に編む.拾い目の始めは, 前身頃のBOからとなる.

仕上げ

糸始末をし, ブロッキングして出来上がり.

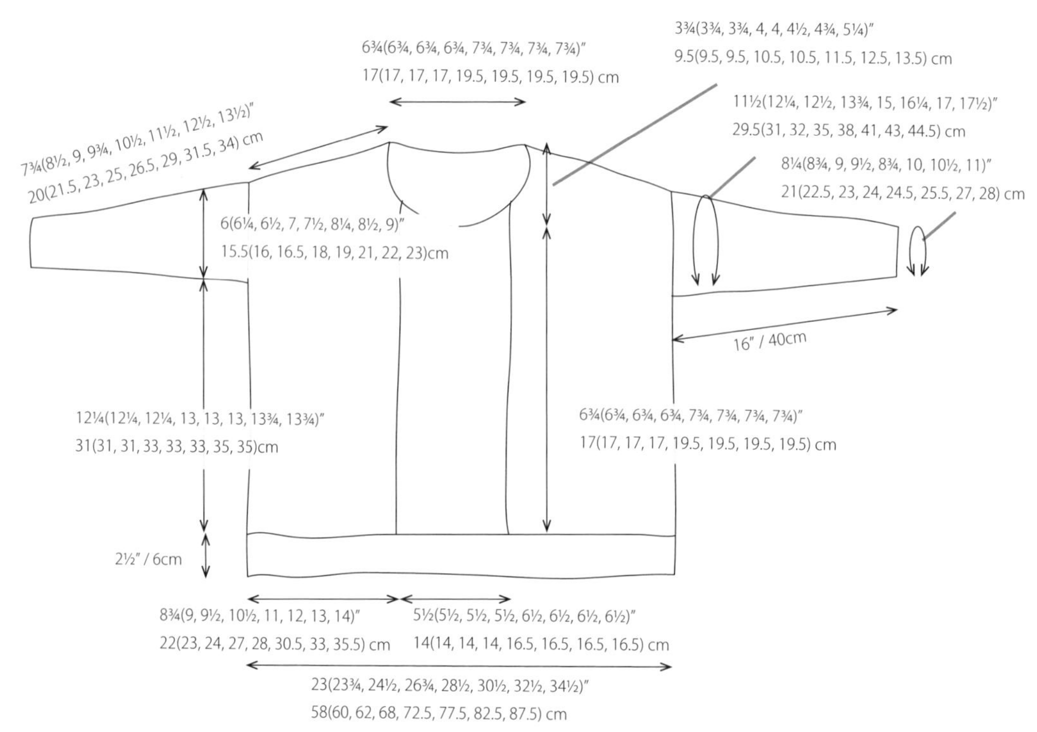

Camellia by Joji Locatelli

Specifications

Yarn

Fingering weight yarn

(MC) Approximately 1415 (1480, 1540, 1775, 1915, 2105, 2335, 2425) yards, 1295 (1355, 1410, 1625, 1755, 1930, 2140, 2220) m.

(CC1) Approximately 120 yards / 110 m.

(CC2) Approximately 120 yards / 110 m.

Quince & Co. Finch (100% wool; 221 yards / 202 m, 50g)

Sample shown in Egret 7 (7, 7, 8, 9, 10, 11, 11) skeins, Dogwood 1 (1, 1, 1, 1, 1) skein, Caspian 1 (1, 1, 1, 1, 1, 1) skein

Needles

A US 4 (3.5 mm) 24" / 60 cm (or longer) circular needle

A US 3 (3.25 mm) 24" / 60 cm (or longer) circular needle

A US 6 (4 mm) straight, DPN or circular needle in any length (for 3 needle bind off)

or needle to obtain gauge

Gauge (after blocking)

26 sts and 38 rows = 4" / 10 cm in St st with US 4 (3.5 mm) needle.

25 sts and 48 rows = 4" / 10 cm in Garter stitch with US 3 (3.25 mm) needle.

Sizes

Finished Chest Measurements: XS (S, M, L, XL, XXL, 3XL, 4XL) = 46 (48, 50, 54, 58, 62, 66, 70)" / 116 (122, 127, 137, 147, 157, 167, 178) cm

Ease: +14" / 35 cm

The sample was knit in size S with 14" / 35 cm positive ease.

Tools

Removable stitch markers, crochet hook, tapestry needle, waste yarn.

Skill Level

Note

Sweater knit in separate pieces from the top down that are later joined together seamlessly.

The striped bands in the front and the back are knit sideways. The rest of the sweater's construction starts at the shoulders and grows towards the back and the front.

When all pieces are complete, the left and right sides are joined to the striped bands with a 3 needle bind off.

The hems, neckband and sleeves are picked up and worked in the round. The sleeves can be knit using magic loop or DPN.

Instructions

Back striped band

With crochet hook and waste yarn, provisionally CO 124 (125, 126, 137, 141, 147, 157, 162) sts onto smaller needle.

Start working with MC.

Stripe pattern set A:

K 2 rows with MC.

K 4 rows with CC1.

Stripe pattern set B

K 2 rows with MC.

K 4 rows with CC2.

Repeat set A & B 4 (4, 4, 4, 5, 5, 5, 5) more times.

Repeat set A once.

K 2 rows with MC.

Break yarn and put all sts on hold using a length of waste yarn.

Front striped band

With crochet hook and waste yarn, provisionally CO 104 (105, 106, 115, 119, 123, 130, 133) sts onto smaller needles.

Start working with MC.

Row 1 (RS): K1, SSK, K to end.

Row 2 (WS): K to end.

Switch to CC1.

Row 3: K1, SSK, K to end.

Row 4: K to end.

Repeat the last 2 rows once.

Work set B once.

Work set A & B 4 (4, 4, 4, 5, 5, 5, 5) times.

Knit 2 rows with MC.

Switch to CC1.

Next row (RS): K1, M1R, K to end.

Next row (WS): K to end.

Repeat the last 2 rows once.

Switch to MC:

Next row (RS): K1, M1R, K to end.

Next row (WS): K to end.

Break yarn and put all sts on hold using a length of waste yarn.

Right back

With larger needles and long tail cast on in MC, CO 53 (56, 58, 64, 69, 75, 82, 88) sts.

Work 2 rows in St st starting with a K row.

Row 3 (RS): Using the cable cast on, CO 4, K to end. 57 (60, 62, 68, 73, 79, 86, 92) sts on the needle. Place a split ring marker between the sts you have just CO and the rest of the sts. This marker will indicate the beginning of the shoulder seam.

Row 4: P to end.

Row 5: K7, W&T.

Row 6: P to end.

Row 7: K to last wrapped st and K it together with wrap, K3, W&T.

Row 8: P to end.

Repeat the last 2 rows 9 (10, 10, 12, 13, 14, 16, 18) more times.

Next row (RS): K to last wrapped st and K it together with wrap, K to end.

Next row: P to end.

Work in St st until work measures 6 (6¼, 6½, 7, 7½, 8¼, 8½, 9" / 15.5 (16, 16.5, 18, 19, 21, 22, 23) cm from your CO edge, measured along the shortest edge (armhole edge), ending with a RS row.

Next row (WS): BO 1 st, P to end.

Do not break yarn and put all sts on hold using a length of waste yarn.

Right front

With larger needles and the WS of the fabric facing you (this will leave an exposed seam look), pick up and knit 53 (56, 58, 64, 69, 75, 82, 88) sts along the right shoulder CO, starting at M you placed when working the right back, and moving towards the armhole edge.

Work 3 rows in St st starting with a knit row.

Next row (WS): P3, W&T.

Next row: K to end.

Next row: P to last wrapped st and P it together with wrap, P3, W&T.

Repeat the last 2 rows 3 (4, 4, 6, 7, 8, 10, 12) more times.

Next row (RS): K to 1 st from end, M1L, K1.

Next row: P to last wrapped st and P it together with wrap, P3, W&T.

Next row: K to end.

Next row: P to last wrapped st and P it together with wrap, P3, W&T.

Repeat the last 4 rows 2 more times.

Next row (RS): K to 1 st from end, M1L, K1. Total 57 (60, 62, 68, 73, 79, 86, 92) sts.

Next row (WS): P to last wrapped st and P it together with wrap, P to end.

Next row (RS): PM at the end of this row. It will indicate the beginning of the front seam. K to end.

Work in St st until work measures 6 (6¼, 6½, 7, 7½, 8¼, 8½, 9" / 15.5 (16, 16.5, 18, 19, 21, 22, 23) cm from your CO edge, measured along the shortest edge (armhole edge), ending with a WS row.

Next row (RS): BO 1 st, K to end.

Next row (WS): P to end.

Break yarn. Put all sts on hold.

Join right side

Place the sts you had on hold for the right back on the needle, and with the yarn you were using K to end of row. Place the sts you had on hold for the right front onto the same needle and knit to end of row. Now both pieces are attached.

Next row (WS): P to end of row.

Work in St st until your piece measures 19¾ (20, 20¼, 22, 22½, 23¼, 24¾, 25¼" / 50.5 (51, 51.5, 56, 57.5, 60, 63, 64.5) cm from your CO edge, measured along the longest edge (neck edge).

BO all sts.

Left back

With larger needles and long tail cast on in MC, CO 53 (56, 58, 64, 69, 75, 82, 88) sts.

Work 3 rows in St st starting with a K row.

Row 4 (WS): Using the cable cast on, CO 4, P to end. 57 (60, 62, 68, 73, 79, 86, 92) sts on the needle. Place a split ring marker between the sts you have just CO and the rest of the sts to indicate the end of the shoulder seam.

Row 5: K to end.

Row 6: P7, W&T.

Row 7: K to end.

Row 8: P to last wrapped st and P it together with wrap, P3, W&T.

Repeat the last 2 rows 9 (10, 10, 12, 13, 14, 16, 18) more times.

Next row (RS): K to end.

Next row: P to last wrapped st and P it together with wrap, P to end.

Work in St st until work measures 6 (6¼, 6½, 7, 7½, 8¼, 8½, 9" / 15.5 (16, 16.5, 18, 19, 21, 22, 23) cm from your CO edge, measured along the shortest edge (armhole edge), ending with a WS row.

Next row (RS): BO 1 st, K to end.

Next row: P to end.

Break yarn. Put all sts on hold.

Left front

With larger needles and the WS of the fabric facing you, pick up and knit 53 (56, 58, 64, 69, 75, 82, 88) sts along the left shoulder CO, starting at the armhole edge and ending at M you placed when working the left back.

Work 2 rows in St st starting with a K row.

Next row (RS): K3, W&T.

Next row: P to end.

Next row: K to last wrapped st and K it together with wrap, K3, W&T.

Next row: P to end.

Repeat the last 2 rows 3 (4, 4, 6, 7, 8, 10, 12) more times.

Next row (RS): K1, M1R, K to last wrapped st and K it together with wrap, K3, W&T.

Next row: P to end.

Next row: K to last wrapped st and K it together with wrap, K3, W&T.

Next row: P to end.

Repeat the last 4 rows 2 more times.

Next row (RS): K1, M1R, k to last wrapped st and K it together with wrap, K to end. Total 57 (60, 62, 68, 73, 79, 86, 92) sts.

Next row (WS): P to end.

Next row (RS): PM at the beginning of this row. It will indicate the beginning of the front seam. K to end.

Work in St st until work measures 6 (6¼, 6½, 7, 7½, 8¼, 8½, 9" / 15.5 (16, 16.5, 18, 19, 21, 22, 23) cm from your CO edge, measured along the shortest edge (armhole edge), ending with a RS row.

Next row (WS): BO 1 st, P to end.

Do not break yarn.

Join left side

K all sts from the left front. Place the sts you had on hold for the left back onto the same needle and K to end of row. Now both pieces are attached.

Next row (WS): P to end of row.

Work in St st until your piece measures 19¾ (20, 20¼, 22, 22½, 23¼, 24¾, 25¼" / 50.5 (51, 51.5, 56, 57.5, 60, 63, 64.5) cm from your CO edge, measured along the longest edge (neck edge).

BO all sts.

Join back

With larger needle, using MC and with the RS of the Right Back piece facing you, pick up and knit 124 (125, 126, 137, 141, 147, 157, 162) sts starting at the neck edge and moving downwards towards the bottom of the garment.

Unravel the provisionally CO sts from the Back Striped Band and place these sts onto a smaller needle.

With both right sides of the fabrics facing each other (the wrong sides should facing you), use a US 6 (4 mm) needle to join the sts you just picked up from the back to the provisional sts from the striped band with a 3 needle bind off. Be careful not to bind off too tightly or else the fabric will be distorted.

With larger needles, MC and the RS of the Left Back piece facing you, pick up and knit 124 (125, 126, 137, 141, 147, 157, 162) sts starting at the bottom edge and moving upwards towards the neck edge.

Place the st you had on hold for the Back Striped Band onto a smaller needle. In the same manner as before, use a US 6 (4 mm) needle to join the sts you picked up from the Left Back to the live sts from the striped band.

Join front

With larger needle, using MC and the RS of the Left Front piece facing you, pick up and knit 104 (105, 106, 115, 119, 123, 130, 133) sts starting at the marker indicating the beginning of the front seam, and moving downwards towards the bottom hem.

Unravel the provisionally CO sts from the Front Striped Band and place these sts onto a smaller needle.

In the same manner as you did for the back, use a US 6 (4 mm) needle to join the sts you just picked up from the front to the provisional sts from the striped band with a 3 needle bind off.

With larger needles, MC and the RS of the Right Front piece facing you, pick up and knit 104 (105, 106, 115, 119, 123, 130, 133) sts along the edge, starting at the bottom hem, and moving towards the marker that indicated the beginning of the front seam.

Place the sts you had on hold for the Front Striped Band onto a smaller needle. In the same manner as before, use a US 6 (4 mm) needle to join the sts you picked up from the Right Front to the live sts from the striped band.

Bottom hem

With smaller needles and the RS facing, MC and starting at the point where the right front meets the right back, pick up and knit 146 (152, 156, 168, 184, 196, 210, 222) sts along the front (1 st for every St st and 1 st for every purl ridge along the striped band) and 146 (152, 156, 168, 184, 196, 210, 222) sts along the back. 292 (304, 312, 336, 368, 392, 420, 444) sts on the needles. PM and join in the round.

Work in Garter st starting with a P round for 2½" / 6 cm.

BO all sts loosely.

Neckband

With smaller needles and the RS facing, MC and starting at the left shoulder seam, pick up and knit approx 72 (74, 74, 74, 78, 80, 82, 84, 86) sts along the front neck and 46 (46, 46, 46, 48, 48, 48, 48) sts along the back neck. PM and join in the round.

Work 10 rounds in Garter st starting with a P round.

BO all sts VERY loosely using larger needles.

Sleeves

With larger needles and starting at the bottom of the armhole opening, pick up and knit 76 (80, 84, 90, 98, 106, 112, 116) sts around it. PM and join in the round.

Work in St st for 12 (10, 10, 9, 7, 6, 6, 5) rounds.

Next round: K1, SSK, K to last 3 sts, K2tog, K1.

Continue working in St st repeating a decrease round every 12 (10, 10, 9, 7, 6, 6, 5) rounds 10 (10, 11, 13, 16, 19, 20, 21) more times. 54 (58, 60, 62, 64, 66, 70, 72) sts on the needle.

Continue working in St st until the sleeve measures 13½" / 34 cm from the armhole, or 2½" / 6 cm less than your desired length.

Change to smaller needle.

Work in Garter st starting with a P round until the cuff measures 2½" / 6 cm.

BO all sts loosely.

Finishing

Weave in ends neatly and block to finished measurements.

詳細情報

Yarn

Fingering weight yarn

(MC)約1415 (1480, 1540, 1775, 1915, 2105, 2335, 2425) yards, 1295 (1355, 1410, 1625, 1755, 1930, 2140, 2220) m

(CC1)約120 yards, 110 m

(CC2)約120 yards, 110 m

Quince & Co. Finch (100% wool; 221 yards/202 m, 50g)

サンプル色は(MC) Egretを7 (7, 7, 8, 9, 10, 11, 11)カセ, (CC1)Dogwoodを1 (1, 1, 1, 1, 1)カセ, (CC2) Caspianを1 (1, 1, 1, 1, 1, 1)カセ

Needles

1 x US4 (3.5 mm) 24" / 60 cm(またはそれより長い)の輪針

1 x US3 (3.25 mm) 24" / 60 cm(またはそれより長い)の輪針

または, ゲージに合わせた太さの針

Gauge (ブロッキング後)

US4 (3.5 mm)の針を使用し, メリヤス編みで26目 & 38段 = 10 cm

US3 (3.25 mm)の針を使用し, ガーター編みで25目 & 48段 = 10 cm

Sizes

出来上がり胸囲寸法 XS (S, M, L, XL, XXL, 3XL, 4XL) = 116 (122, 127, 137, 147, 157, 167, 178) cm

余裕 +35 cm.

モデルはSサイズを着用し, 余裕 として+35 cm.

Tools

段数マーカー , かぎ針, 綴じ針, 別糸

Skill Level

Note

セーターはトップダウンで身頃を別々に編んでから, はぎ目が目立たないようつないでいく.

前後身頃のストライプバンドは横方向に, ストライプバンドを挟んだ右前後身頃, 左前後身頃はそれぞれ肩から裾に向けて編んでいく.全てを編み終えてから左右身頃の端とストライプバンドを引き抜きはぎでつなげる.裾, 襟, 袖は身頃から目を拾い, 輪で編む.袖はマジックループでも4本針でも編める.

編みかた

後ろストライプバンド

かぎ針と別糸を用い, かぎ針を用いた後でほどける作り目で小さい方のサイズの編み針でCO 124 (125, 126, 137, 141, 147, 157, 162)目.

MCで編み始める.

ストライプパターン　セットA

2段をMCで全てK.

4段をCC1全てK.

ストライプパターン　セットB

2段をMCで全てK.

4段をCC2全てK.

このセットA & Bを, さらに4 (4, 4, 4, 5, 5, 5, 5)回編む.

セットAを1回編む.

2段をMCで全てK.

糸を切る.全ての目を別糸に休める.

前ストライプバンド

かぎ針と別糸を用い, かぎ針を用いた後でほどける作り目で小さい方のサイズの編み針でCO104(105, 106, 115, 119, 123, 130, 133)目.

MCで編み始める.

段1(RS): K1, SSK, 最後までK.

段2(WS): 全てK.

CC1に持ちかえる.

段3: K1, SSK, 最後までK.

段4: 全てK.

最後の2段をもう1回編む.

セットBを1回編む.

ストライプパターン　セットA & Bを, 4 (4, 4, 4, 5, 5, 5, 5)回編む.

2段をMCで全てK.

CC1に持ちかえる.

次の段(RS): K1, M1R, 最後までK.

次の段(WS): 全てK.

最後の2段をもう1回編む.

MCに持ちかえる.

次の段(RS): K1, M1R, 最後までK.

次の段(WS): 全てK.

糸を切る.全ての目を別糸に休める.

右後ろ身頃

太い方の編み針で, MCを使い指で掛ける作り目でCO53(56, 58, 64, 69, 75, 82, 88)目.

K段で始めるメリヤス編みで2段編む.

段3(RS): Cable cast onでCO4, 最後までK.

計57 (60, 62, 68, 73, 79, 86, 92)目.

CO4と元の目の間にMを付ける.このMが肩のシームの開始位置になる.

段4: 全てP.

段5: K7, W＆T.

段6: 全てP.

段7: 最後にラップした目までK, ラップと目を一緒にK, K3, W&T.

段8: 全てP.

最後の2段をさらに9 (10, 10, 12, 13, 14, 16, 18)回編む.

次の段(RS): 最後にラップした目までK, ラップと目を一緒にK, 最後までK.

次の段: 全てP.

メリヤス編みで, 作り目から短い方の長さ(袖ぐり側)が15.5(16, 16.5, 18, 19, 21, 22, 23) cmになるまで編む.RSで編み終える.

次の段(WS): BO1, 最後までP.

糸は切らない.全ての目を別糸に休ませる.

右前身頃

太い方の編み針で, WSを見ながら右後ろ身頃のMから袖ぐりの方に向かって, 右肩に沿って作り目（これが肩のシームになる）から53(56, 58, 64, 69, 75, 82, 88)目拾う.

K段で始めるメリヤス編みで3段編む.

次の段(WS): P3, W&T.

次の段: 全てK.

次の段: 最後のラップまでP, ラップと目を一緒にP, P3, W&T.

最後の2段をさらに3 (4, 4, 6, 7, 8, 10, 12)回編む.

次の段(RS): 最後の1目前までK, M1L, K1.

次の段: 最後のラップまでP, ラップと目を一緒にP, P3, W&T.

次の段: 全てK.

次の段: 最後のラップまでP, ラップと目を一緒にP, P3, W&T.

最後の4段をさらに2回編む.

次の段(RS): 最後の1目前までK, M1L, K1.

計57 (60, 62, 68, 73, 79, 86, 92)目.

次の段(WS): 最後のラップまでP, ラップと目を一緒にP, 最後までP.

次の段(RS): この段の最後の目にPM.このMが前身頃はぎ合わせの開始位置になる.最後までK.

メリヤス編みで作り目から短い方の長さ(袖ぐり側)が15.5(16, 16.5, 18, 19, 21, 22, 23) cmになるまで編む.編み終わりはWS.

次の段(RS): BO1, 最後までK.

次の段(WS): 全てP.

糸を切る.全ての目を別糸に休ませる.

右側前後身頃をつなげる

右後ろ身頃の休めていた目を編み針に移し, 切らずに残していた糸を使って全てK.右前身頃の休めていた目を同じ編み針に移し, 続けてK.これで前後身頃が一緒になる.

次の段(WS): 全てP.

メリヤス編みで, 作り目から長い方の長さ（襟ぐり側）が, 50.5(51, 51.5, 56, 57.5, 60, 63, 64.5) cmになるまで編む.

全てBO.

左後ろ身頃

太い方の編み針に指で掛ける作り目でMCを使ってCO53(56, 58, 64, 69, 75, 82, 88)目.

K段で始めるメリヤス編みで3段編む.

段4(WS): Cable cast onでCO4, 最後までP.CO4と元の目の間にMを付ける.このMが肩のシームの終わり位置になる.

計57 (60, 62, 68, 73, 79, 86, 92)目.

段5: 全てK.

段6: P7, W&T.

段7: 全てK.

段8: 最後のラップまでP, ラップと目を一緒にP, P3, W&T.

最後の2段をさらに9 (10, 10, 12, 13, 14, 16, 18)回編む.

次の段(RS): 全てK.

次の段: 最後のラップまでP, ラップと目を一緒にP, 最後までP.

メリヤス編みで, 作り目から短い方の長さ（袖ぐり側）が, 15.5(16, 16.5, 18, 19, 21, 22, 23) cmになるまで編む.編み終わりはWS.

次の段(RS): BO1, 残りをK.

次の段: 全てP.

糸を切る.全ての目を別糸に休める.

左前身頃

太い方の編み針で, WSを見ながら袖ぐり側から左後ろ身頃のMに向かって, 左肩に沿って作り目から53(56, 58, 64, 69, 75, 82, 88)目拾う.

K段で始めるメリヤス編みで2段編む.

次の段(RS): K3, W&T.

次の段: 全てP.

次の段: 最後のラップまでK, ラップと目を一緒にK, K3, W&T.

次の段: 全てP.

最後の2段をさらに3 (4, 4, 6, 7, 8, 10, 12)回編む.

次の段(RS): K1, M1R, 最後のラップまでK, ラップと目を一緒にK, K3, W&T.

次の段: 全てP.

次の段: K1, M1R, 最後のラップまでK, ラップと目を一緒にK, K3, W&T.

次の段: 全てP.

最後の4段をさらに2回編む.

次の段(RS): K1, M1R, 最後のラップまでK, ラップと目を一緒にK, 最後までK.

計57 (60, 62, 68, 73, 79, 86, 92)目.

次の段(WS): 全てP.

次の段(RS): この段の最初の目にPM.ここは前身頃のはぎ合わせ開始位置になる.全てK.

メリヤス編みで, 作り目から短い方の長さ（袖ぐり側）が, 15.5(16, 16.5, 18, 19, 21, 22, 23) cmになるまで編む.編み終わりはRS.

次の段(WS): BO1, 最後までP.

糸は切らない.

左側前後身頃をつなげる

左前身頃の目を全てK.左後ろ身頃の休ませていた目を同じ編み針に移し, 全てK.これで前後身頃が一緒になる.

次の段(WS): 全てP.

メリヤス編みで, 作り目から長い方の長さ（襟ぐり側）が, 50.5(51, 51.5, 56, 57.5, 60, 63, 64.5) cmになるまで編む.

全てBO.

後ろ身頃をはぎ合わせる

大きい方のサイズの編み針を使ってMCで, 右後ろ身頃のRSを見ながら, 襟ぐりから裾に向かって124(125, 126, 137, 141, 147, 157, 162)目拾う.

後ろストライプバンドの別糸の作り目をほどきながら小さい方のサイズの編み針に移す.

両方のRSが中表になるようにして(それぞれのWSが外側), かぎ針を使い後ろ身頃から拾った目とストライプバンドの別糸からほどいた目を引き抜きはぎではぎあわせる.出来上がりが歪んでしまうので, はいだ目がきつくなりすぎないように気をつける.

大きいサイズの編み針にMCで, 左後ろ身頃のRSを見ながら, 裾から襟ぐりにむけて124(125, 126, 137, 141, 147, 157, 162)目拾う.

休ませていた後ろストライプバンドの目を小さいサイズの編み針に移す.右後ろ身頃と同じように, 左後ろ身頃の拾った目とストライプバンドの休めていた目を引き抜きはぎではぎあわせる.

前身頃をはぎ合わせる

大きいサイズの編み針を使ってMCで, 左前身頃のRSを見ながら, 前身頃のはぎ合わせ開始位置のMから裾に向かって104(105, 106, 115, 119, 123, 130, 133)目拾う.

前ストライプバンドの別糸の作り目をほどきながら小さいサイズの編み針に移す.

後ろ身頃のはぎ合わせ同様にかぎ針を使い, 前身頃から拾った目とストライプバンドの別糸からほどいた目を引き抜きはぎではぎあわせる.

大きいサイズの編み針を使ってMCで, 右前身頃のRSをみながら, 裾から前身頃のはぎ合わせ終了位置のMに向かって104(105, 106, 115, 119, 123, 130, 133)目拾う.

休ませていた前ストライプバンドの目を小さいサイズの編み針に移す.後ろ身頃と同様にかぎ針で右前身頃の拾った目と, 前ストライプバンドの休ませた目と引き抜きはぎではぎあわせる.

裾

小さいサイズの編み針を使ってRSをみながら, MCで右前身頃と右後ろ身頃のはぎ合わせ位置から始めて, 前身頃から146(152, 156, 168, 184, 196, 210, 222)目を, 後ろ身頃から292(304, 312, 336, 368, 392, 420, 444)目を拾う.拾い目は前ストライプのバンドの裏編みの畝から1目, メリヤス編みの1目から1目を拾うようにする.

計292 (304, 312, 336, 368, 392, 420, 444)目.

PM, 輪で編み進める.

P周で始めるガーター編みで6cm編む.

きつくならないように緩めにBO.

襟

小さなサイズの編み針を使ってRSを見ながら, MCで肩のシームの位置から始めて襟ぐりに沿って, 前身頃から72(74, 74, 74, 78, 80, 82, 84, 86)目, 後ろ身頃から46(46, 46, 46, 48, 48, 48, 48)目拾う.

PM, 輪で編み進める.

P周で始めるガーター編みで10周編む.

大きなサイズの編み針できつくならないように緩めにBO.

袖

大きなサイズの編み針で, 脇下中心から始めて76(80, 84, 90, 98, 106, 112, 116)目拾う.

PM, 輪で編み進める.

メリヤス編みで12(10, 10, 9, 7, 6, 6, 5)周編む.

次の周(減目周): K1, SSK, 最後から3目前までK, K2tog, K1.

メリヤス編みを続けながら, 減目周を12(10, 10, 9, 7, 6, 6, 5)周毎に, さらに10(10, 11, 13, 16, 19, 20, 21)回編む.

計54(58, 60, 62, 64, 66, 70, 72)目.

メリヤス編みで脇下から34cm, または希望の長さより6cm短い長さまで編む.

小さいサイズの編み針に持ちかえる.

P周で始めるガーター編みで袖口を6cm編む.

きつくならないように緩めにBO.

仕上げ

糸始末をし, 出来上がり寸法になるようブロッキングする.

Botan by Helen Stewart

Specifications

Yarn

Fingering weight yarn

(MC) Approximately 420 yards, 384 m

(CC) Approximately 104 yards, 95 m

(MC) Madelinetosh Tosh merino light (100 % Merino; 420 yards / 384 m, 115g)

(CC) Madelinetosh Unicorn tails (100 % Merino; 52 yards / 48 m)

Sample shown in (MC) Holi Festival 1 skein, (CC) Pop Rocks 2 skeins

Needles

A US 6 (4 mm) 32" / 80 cm (or longer) circular needle

or needle to obtain gauge

Gauge (after blocking)

18 sts & 30 rows = 4" / 10 cm in Garter stitch with US 6 (4 mm) needle

Sizes

Finished measurements: 40" / 102 cm long x 15¾" / 40 cm wide

Tools

Tapestry needle

Skill Level

Stitch Guide

MB (Make Bobble)

(K1, P1, K1, P1, K1, P1) into next stitch. With the left needle lift second, third, fourth, fifth and sixth stitches over the first stitch one at a time and off the needle.

I-cord bind off

On left needle, CO 3 sts, using the cable cast on method. *K2, SSK, slip 3 sts from right needle to left; repeat from * until you have 3 sts remaining.

At the end of your work, replace the 3 sts on your left needle and K3tog tbl.

Note

This shawl is worked flat in garter stich from upper right tip towards the left edge. Work picot sections with MC and bobble section with CC while shaping the shawl. Carry MC along the side all the way. Finishing it off with I-code bind off.

Instructions

Set up

Note: You might notice a gap between the tubular edge and the body of the shawl at the beginning of your work. This is normal and you can use the tail to close this up when you are finishing.

Using MC, with knitted cast on or long tail cast on, CO 3 sts.

Row 1 (RS): K1, Sl1 wyf, K1.

Row 2 (WS): Sl1 wyf, K1, Sl1 wyf.

Row 3 (RS): K1, Sl1 wyf, K1.

Row 4 (WS): CO 1 st using backward loop cast on, Kfb (into CO st), Sl1 wyf, K1, Sl1 wyf. Total 5 sts.

Row 5 (RS): K1, Sl1 wyf, K1, YO, K2. Total 6 sts.

Row 6 (WS): K to last 4 sts, Kfb, Sl1 wyf, K1, Sl1 wyf. 7 sts.

Row 7 (RS): K1, Sl1 wyf, K1, YO, K to end. Total 8 sts.

Row 8 (WS): K to last 4 sts, Kfb, Sl1 wyf, K1, Sl1 wyf. 9 sts.

Row 9 (RS): K1, Sl1 wyf, K1, YO, K to end. Total 10 sts.

Row 10 (WS): K to last 4 sts, Kfb, Sl1 wyf, K1, Sl1 wyf. Total 11 sts.

Row 11 (RS): K1, Sl1 wyf, K1, YO, K to last 3 sts, K2tog, K1.

Row 12 (WS): K to last 4 sts, Kfb, Sl1 wyf, K1, Sl1 wyf. Total 12 sts.

Wide Picot Section

With MC

Row 1 (RS): K1, Sl1 wyf, K1, YO, K to last 3 sts, K2tog, K1. Total 12 sts.

Row 2 (WS): K to last 4 sts, Kfb, Sl1 wyf, K1, Sl1 wyf. 13 sts.

Row 3 - 6: Repeat rows 1 - 2 for 2 more times ending in WS row. Total 15 sts.

Row 7 (RS): Repeat row 1 once more.

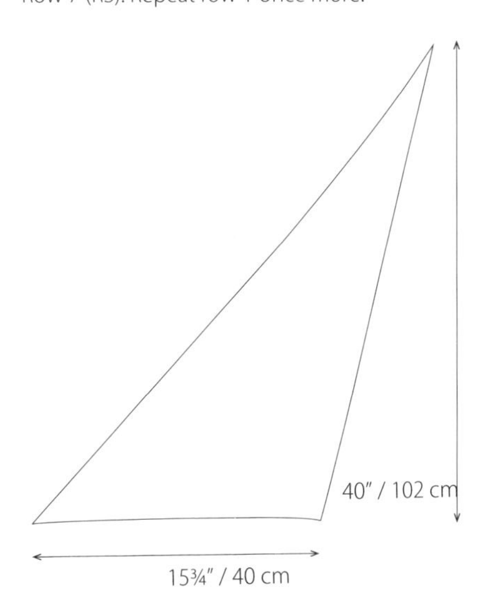

Row 8 (WS): CO 2 sts using cable cast on, BO 2 sts, K to last 4 sts, Kfb, Sl1 wyf, K1, Sl1 wyf. Total 16 sts.

Repeat rows 1 - 8, 4 more times ending in WS row. 32 sts.

Repeat rows 1 - 6, once more. Total 35 sts.

There is a total of 46 rows in this section.

Bobble Section

With CC

Row 1 (RS): K1, Sl1 wyf, K1, YO, K to last 3 sts, K2tog, K1. (Carry MC along side)

Row 2 (WS): CO 2 sts using cable cast on, BO 2 sts, *K5, MB* to last 10 sts, K6, Kfb, Sl1 wyf, K1, Sl1 wyf. 36 sts.

Break CC.

Repeat [Previous Instructions – Wide Picot & Bobble section] 3 more times. Total 108 sts.

Medium Picot Section

With MC

Row 1 (RS): K1, Sl1 wyf, K1, YO, K to last 3 sts, K2tog, K1. Total 108 sts.

Row 2 (WS): K to last 4 sts, Kfb, Sl1 wyf, K1, Sl1 wyf. Total 109 sts.

Row 3 - 6: Repeat rows 1 - 2 for 2 more times ending in WS row. Total 111 sts.

Row 7 (RS): Repeat row 1 once more.

Row 8 (WS): CO 2 sts using cable cast on, BO 2 sts, K to last 4 sts, Kfb, Sl1 wyf, K1, Sl1 wyf. Total 112 sts.

Repeat rows 1 - 8, once more ending in WS row. 116 sts.

Repeat rows 1 - 6, once more. Total 119 sts.

There is a total of 22 rows in this section.

Repeat Bobble Section once. Total 120 sts.

Repeat Medium Picot section once. Total 131 sts.

Repeat Bobble Section once more. Total 132 sts.

Narrow Picot Section

With MC

Row 1 (RS): K1, Sl1 wyf, K1, YO, K to last 3 sts, K2tog, K1. Total 132 sts.

Row 2 (WS): K to last 4 sts, Kfb, Sl1 wyf, K1, Sl1 wyf. Total 133 sts.

Row 3 - 6: Repeat rows 1 - 2 for 2 more times ending in WS row. Total 135 sts.

Penultimate Bobble Section

With CC

Row 1 (RS): K1, Sl1 wyf, K1, YO, K to last 3 sts, K2tog, K1. (Carry MC along side)

Row 2 (WS): CO 2 sts using cable cast on, BO 2 sts, *K5, MB* to last 8 sts, K4, Kfb, Sl1 wyf, K1, Sl1 wyf. 136 sts.

Break CC. Total 136 sts.

Repeat Narrow Picot Section once more. Total 139 sts

Break MC.

Final Bobble Section

With CC

Row 1 (RS): K1, Sl1 wyf, K1, YO, K to last 3 sts, K2tog, K1.

Row 2 (WS): CO 2 sts using cable cast on, BO 2 sts, *K5, MB* to last 12 sts, K8, Kfb, Sl1 wyf, K1, Sl1 wyf. 140 sts.

With CC, BO all sts using I-cord bind off.

Finishing

Weave in ends, closing any gap between I-cord and body of shawl at beginning of shawl.

Blocking

Soak in lukewarm water for 20 minutes. Gently squeeze out excess water and roll in a towel. Lay flat on blocking surface (mats or a bed work well) and using either blocking wires or pins stretch into shape. Let the shawl dry completely before unpinning.

詳細情報

Yarn

Fingering weight yarn, (MC) 約420 yards, 384 m, (CC) 約104 yards, 95 m

(MC) Madelinetosh tosh merino light (100 % Merino; 420 yards / 384 m, 115g) , (CC) Madelinetosh Unicorn tails (100 % Merino; 52 yards / 48 m)

サンプル色は, (MC) Holi Festival 1 カセ, (CC) Pop Rocks 2 カセ

Needles

1 × US 6 (4 mm) 32" / 80 cm 又はそれ以上の長さの輪針またはゲージに合わせた太さの針

Gauge (ブロッキング後)

US 6 (4 mm)を使用, ガーター編みで18目 & 30段 = 10 cm

Sizes

出来上がり寸法:長さ102 cm x 幅40 cm

Tools

綴じ針

Skill Level

Stitch Guide

MB (Make Bobble, ボッブルを編む)

次の1目に(K1, P1, K1, P1, K1, P1)を編み入れる. 左針を使って, 2, 3, 4, 5, 6番目の目を持ち上げて一度に最初の目に被せる.

I-code bind off

左針にCable cast onでCO3目.*K2, SSK.右針から左針に3目を滑らせる.*からを, 残りの目が3目になるまで繰り返す.左針に移し, K3tog tbl.

Note

右の先端から左のエッジに向かってガーター編みで編むショール. MCでピコット部分＋CCでボッブル部分の組み合わせを目数を増やしながら編んでいく. MCの糸は切らない.

編みかた

セットアップ

MCを使用し, Knitted cast onまたは指で掛ける作り目でCO 3目.

Note: ショールの編み始めで, 端の部分と本体の間に穴ができる場合があるが, 仕上げの際に調整することが可能.

段1 (RS): K1, Sl1 wyf, K1.

段2 (WS): Sl1 wyf, K1, Sl1 wyf.

段3 (RS): K1, Sl1 wyf, K1.

段4 (WS): 巻増し目で, CO 1目, COの目にKfb, Sl1 wyf, K1, Sl1 wyf. 5目.

段5 (RS): K1, Sl1 wyf, K1, YO, K2. 6目.

段6 (WS): 最後から4目前までK, Kfb, Sl1 wyf, K1, Sl1 wyf. 7目 .

段7 (RS): K1, Sl1 wyf, K1, YO, 最後までK. 8目.

段8 (WS): 最後から4目前までK, Kfb, Sl1 wyf, K1, Sl1 wyf. 9目.

段9 (RS): K1, Sl1 wyf, K1, YO, 最後までK. 10目.

段10 (WS): 最後から4目前までK, Kfb, Sl1 wyf, K1, Sl1 wyf. 11目.

段11 (RS): K1, Sl1 wyf, K1, YO, 最後から3目前までK, K2tog, K1.

段12 (WS): 最後の4目前までK, Kfb, Sl1 wyf, K1, Sl1 wyf. 12目.

ワイドピコットセクション

MCで編む.

段1 (RS): K1, Sl1 wyf, K1, YO, 最後の3目前までK, K2tog, K1. 12目.

段2 (WS): 最後の4目前までK, Kfb, Sl1 wyf, K1, Sl1 wyf. 13目.

段3 - 6: 段1 - 2をあと2回編む, 編み終わりはWS. 15目.

段7 (RS): 段1を編む.

段8 (WS): Cable cast onでCO 2目, BO 2目, 最後の4目前までK, Kfb, Sl1 wyf, K1, Sl1 wyf. 16目.

段1 - 8をあと4回編む, 編み終わりはWS. 32目.

段1 - 6を1回編む. 35目.

ここまで. 46段.

ボッブルセクション

CCで編む.

段1 (RS): K1, Sl1 wyf, K1, YO, 最後の3目前までK, K2tog, K1. (MCは横に置いておく)

段2 (WS): Cable cast onでCO 2目, BO 2目, *K5, MB*を最後から10目前まで繰り返す, K6, Kfb, Sl1 wyf, K1, Sl1 wyf. 36目.

CCを切る.

前述のワイドピコットとボッボルセクションをあと3回編む. 108目.

ミディアムピコットセクション

MCで編む.

段1 (RS): K1, Sl1 wyf, K1, YO, 最後の3目前までK, K2tog, K1. 108目.

段2 (WS): 最後の4目前までK, Kfb, Sl1 wyf, K1, Sl1 wyf. 109目.

段3 - 6: 段1 - 2をあと2回編む, 編み終わりはWS. 111目.

段7 (RS): 段1を編む.

段8 (WS): Cable cast onでCO 2目, BO 2目, 最後の4目前までK, Kfb, Sl1 wyf, K1, Sl1 wyf. 112目.

段1 - 8をあと1回編む, 編み終わりはWS. 116目.

段1 - 6をあと1回編む. 119目.

このセクション. 22段.

ボッブルセクションを1回編む. 120目.

ミディアムピコットセクションを1回編む. 131目.

ボッブルセクションを1回編む. 132目.

細いピコットセクション

MCで編む.

段1 (RS): K1, Sl1 wyf, K1, YO, 最後の3目前までK, K2tog, K1. 132目.

段2 (WS): 最後の4目前までK, Kfb, Sl1 wyf, K1, Sl1 wyf. 133目.

段3 - 6: 段1 - 2 をあと2回編む, 編み終わりはWS. 135目.

最後から２回目のボッブルセクション

CCで編む.

段1 (RS): K1, Sl1 wyf, K1, YO, 最後の3目前までK, K2tog, K1. (MCは横に置いておく)

段2 (WS): Cable cast onでCO 2目, BO 2目, *K5, MB*を最後の8目前まで繰り返す, K4, Kfb, Sl1 wyf, K1, Sl1 wyf. 136目.

CCを切る. 136目.

細いピコットセクションをあと1回編む. 139目.

MCを切る.

最後のボッブルセクション

CCで編む.

段1 (RS): K1, Sl1 wyf, K1, YO, 最後の3目前までK, K2tog, K1.

段2 (WS): Cable cast onでCO 2目, BO 2目, *K5, MB*を最後から12目前まで繰り返す, K8, Kfb, Sl1 wyf, K1, Sl1 wyf.計140目.

全ての目をCCを用い, I-cord bind offでBO.

仕上げ

ショールの編み始め部分のi-codeと本体の間の穴を埋めるように, 糸始末をする.

ブロッキング

ぬるま湯に20分浸ける.優しく水を絞り, タオルでくるむ.平らに広げる(マットやベッドの上が良い).ブロッキングワイヤーやピンを使って形を整える.完全に乾いてからピンを外す.

Wisteria by Amy Christoffers

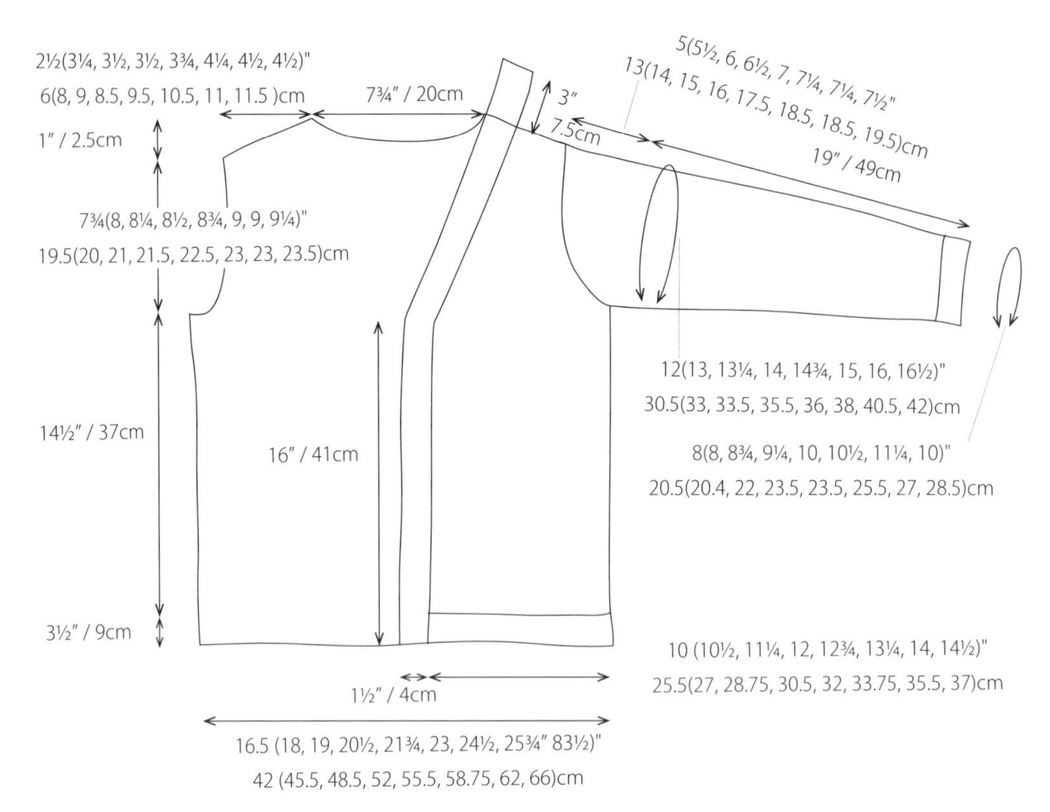

Specifications

Yarn

Sport weight yarn

Approximately 1200 (1300, 1350, 1400, 1500, 1600, 1700, 1800) yards, 1097 (1189, 1234, 1280, 1371, 1463, 1554, 1646) m

8 (9, 9, 10, 10, 11, 12, 13) balls of Berroco Corsica (90% Cotton, 10% Cashmere; 150 yards / 137 m, 50g)

Sample is shown in 3619 Fig

Needles

A US 3 (3.25 mm) 24" / 60 cm (or longer) circular needle or straight needles

A US 5 (3.75 mm) 24" / 60 cm (or longer) circular needle or straight needles

or needles to obtain gauge

Gauge (after blocking)

24 sts & 26 rows = 4" / 10 cm in St st with US 5 (3.75 mm) needle

Sizes

Finished Chest Measurements:

XS (S, M, L, XL, 2XL, 3XL, 4XL) = 34 (36, 39, 42, 44, 47, 50, 52)" / 86.5 (91.5, 99, 106.5, 112, 119.5, 127, 132) cm

Ease: +2-4" / 5-10cm

The sample was knit in size S with 2" / 5 cm positive ease.

Tools

Tapestry needle, removable stitch markers (5), buttons (1.8 cm x 5)

Skill Level

Note

This cardigan in worked in pieces and seamed. The sleeves are knitted flat and seamed into place. The garter front bands are worked as you go.

Instructions

Back

With smaller needles, using long tail cast on, CO 101 (109, 117, 125, 133, 141, 149, 157) sts.

Set up row (WS): P1, *K1, P1; rep from * to end.

Work in 1x1 rib as established for 28 rows, ending with a WS row.

Change to larger needle.

Set up pattern

Row 1 (RS): K1, *K1, YO, SSK, P1; rep from * to 4 sts before end, K1, YO, SSK, K1.

Row 2, 4, 6, 8 (WS): P4, *K1, P3; rep from * to 1 st before end, P1.

Row 3: K1, *K1, K2tog, YO, P1; rep from * to 4 sts before end, K1, K2tog, YO, K1.

Row 5: K1, *K2toq, YO, K1, P1; rep from * to 4 sts before end, K2tog, YO, K2.

Row 7: K1, *YO, SSK, K1, P1; rep from * to 4 sts before end, YO, SSK, K2.

Work in pattern, repeating rows 1-8 until piece measures 18" / 46 cm from CO edge, ending with WS row.

Shape Armhole

Note: As the stitches are decreased there may not be enough stitches to work the patterns corresponding YO and decrease. When there are no longer enough stitches to work in pattern, work the remaining stitches in St st.

BO 6 (6, 7, 8, 9, 10, 11, 12) sts at the beginning of the next 2 rows.

Decrease row (RS): K1, K2tog, work in patterns as established to 3 sts before end, SSK, K1. 2 sts decreased.

All WS rows: Work as established.

Repeat decrease row 5 (5, 6, 9, 10, 11, 12, 14) times more.

Total 77 (85, 89, 89, 93, 97, 101, 103) sts.

Work even until piece measures 7¾ (8, 8¼, 8½, 8¾, 9, 9, 9¼)" / 19.5 (20, 21, 21.5, 22, 23, 23, 23.5) cm from BO row.

Shape shoulders

BO 5 (6, 7, 7, 7, 8, 9, 9) sts at the beginning of the next 4 rows, then 4 (6, 6, 6, 8, 8, 8, 9) sts at the beginning of the next 2 rows. Total 49 sts.

BO remaining sts for neck back.

Left Front

With smaller needles, using long tail cast on, CO 59 (63, 67, 71, 75, 79, 83, 87) sts.

Set up row (WS): K10 *P1, K1; rep from * to 1 st before end, P1.

Next row: Work in 1x1 rib as established to 10 sts before end, K to end.

Work as established for 27 rows, ending with a WS row.

Change to larger needle.

Set up pattern

Row 1 (RS): K1, *P1, K1, YO, SSK; rep from * to 10 sts before end, K10.

Rows 2, 4, 6, 8 (WS): K10, *P3, K1; rep from * to 1 st before end, P1.

Row 3 (RS): K1, *P1, K1, K2tog, YO; rep from * to 10 sts before end, K10.

Row 5 (RS): K1, *P1, K2tog, YO, K1; rep from * to 10 sts before end, K10.

Row 7 (RS): K1, *P1, YO, SSK, K1; rep from * to 10 sts before end, K10.

Work in pattern, repeating rows 1-8 until piece measures 16" / 41 cm from CO edge, ending with WS row.

Shape Neck

Decrease row (RS): Work as established to 11 sts before the end of the row, K2tog, K9. 1 st decreased.

All WS rows: K10, work as established to the end of the row.

Repeat the neck edge decrease on next RS row twice, then at [4th row once, next RS row once], repeat[ ] 9 more times.

AT THE SAME TIME, when body measures 18" / 46 cm, ending with WS row, BO 6 (6, 7, 8, 9, 10, 11, 12) sts at the beginning of the next row.

Work 1 WS row.

Shape Armhole

Decrease row (RS): K1, K2tog, work in patterns as established to the end of the row. 1 st decreased.

Repeat the arm edge decrease row 5 (5, 6, 9, 10, 11, 12, 14) times more.

Total 24 (28, 30, 30, 32, 34, 36, 37) sts.

Work even until piece measures 7¾ (8, 8¼, 8½, 8¾, 9, 9, 9¼)" / 19.5 (20, 21, 21.5, 22, 23, 23, 23.5) cm from the underarm BO row ending with a WS row.

Shape shoulders

BO 5 (6, 7, 7, 7, 8, 9, 9) sts at the beginning of the next 2 RS rows, then 4 (6, 6, 6, 8, 8, 8, 9) sts at the beginning of the next RS row. Total 10 sts.

Neck extension

Next row (WS): K10, CO 1st for selvedge, using the backwards loop cast on. Total 11 sts.

Work in garter stitch as established for 30 rows. BO all sts.

Place 5 removable markers on front band to indicate placement of buttons.

PM for 1st button from 2.5" / 5 cm or 19th row from CO edge and 5th button around the first row of neck shaping. Divide evenly between 1st and 5th buttons to mark 3 more buttons.

In correspondence with the position of markers to make the button holes in right front band.

Right Front

With smaller needles, using long tail cast on, CO 59 (63, 67, 71, 75, 79, 83, 87) sts.

Set up row (WS): *P1, K1; rep from * to 11 sts before end, P1, K10.

Next row: K10, work in 1x1 rib as established to end.

Work as established for 2.5" / 5 cm or 18th row from CO edge, ending with a WS row.

Buttonhole row: K4, K2tog, YO, work to end as established.

Note: from here on, buttonhole row is not mentioned in the pattern. Keep working on 4 more buttonhole rows in correspondence of markers on left front band.

AT THE SAME TIME continue to work as established for 11 more rows, ending with a WS row.

Change to larger needle.

Set up pattern

Row 1 (RS): K10, *K1, YO, SSK, P1; rep from * to 1 st before end, K1.

Rows 2, 4, 6, 8 (WS): P1, *K1, P3; rep from * to 10 sts before end, K10.

Row 3: K10, *K1, K2tog, YO, P1; rep from * to 1 st before end, K1.

Row 5: K10, *K2tog, YO, K1, P1; rep from * to 1 st before end, K1.

Row 7: K10, *YO, SSK, K1, P1; rep from * to 1 st before end, K1.

Work in pattern, repeating rows 1-8 until piece measures 16" / 41 cm from CO edge, ending with WS row.

Shape Neck

Decrease row (RS): K9, SSK, work as established to the end of the row. 1 st decreased.

All WS rows: Work as established to 10 sts before end, K10.

Repeat the neck edge decrease every RS row twice, then at [4th row once, next RS row once], repeat [] 9 more times.

AT THE SAME TIME, when body measures the same as for the back, shape the armhole, ending with a RS row, BO 6 (6, 7, 8, 9, 10, 11, 12) sts at the beginning of the next row.

Decrease row (RS): Work in patterns as established to 3 sts before end, SSK, K1. 1 st decreased.

Repeat the arm edge decrease every RS row 5 (5, 6, 9, 10, 11, 12, 14) times more.

Work even over remaining 24 (28, 30, 30, 32, 34, 36, 37) sts until piece measures 7¾ (8, 8¼, 8½, 8¾, 9, 9, 9¼)"/ 19.5 (20, 21, 21.5, 22, 23, 23, 23.5) cm from BO row ending with a RS row.

Shape shoulders

BO 5 (6, 7, 7, 7, 8, 9, 9) sts at the beginning of the next 2 WS rows, then 4 (6, 6, 6, 8, 8, 8, 9) sts at the beginning of the next WS row. Total 10 sts.

Neck extension

Next row (RS): K10, CO 1 st for selvedge, using the backwards loop cast on. Total 11 sts. Work in garter stitch as established for 29 rows. BO all sts.

Sleeves

With smaller needles, using long tail cast on, CO 49 (49, 53, 57, 57, 61, 65, 69) sts.

Set up row (WS): *P1, K1; repeat from * to 1 st before end, P1.

Work in 1x1 rib as established for 22 rows, ending with a WS row.

Change to larger needle.

Set up pattern

Row 1 (RS): K1, *K1, YO, SSK, P1; rep from * to 4 sts before end, K1, YO, SSK, K1.

Rows 2, 4, 6, 8 (WS): P4, *K1, P3; rep from * to 1 st before end, P1.

Row 3: K1, *K1, K2tog, YO, P1; rep from * to 4 sts before end, K1, K2tog, YO, K1.

Row 5: K1, *K2tog, YO, K1, P1; rep from * to 4 sts before end, K2tog, YO, K2.

Row 7: K1, *YO, SSK, K1, P1; rep from * to 4 sts before end, YO, SSK, K2.

Increase Row: K1, M1, work as established to 1 st before end, M1, K1. 2 sts increased.

Rep the increase row every 8th (6th, 6th, 6th, 6th, 6th, 8th) row 11 (14, 13, 13, 14, 14, 15, 15) times more. Total 73 (79, 81, 85, 87, 91, 97, 101) sts.

Continue working in pattern as established until piece measures 19" / 49 cm from CO edge, ending with WS row.

Shape Sleeve cap

BO 6 (6, 7, 8, 9, 10, 11, 12) sts at the beginning of the next 2 rows.

Work decrease row as follows:

(RS): K1, K2tog, work in patterns as established to 3 sts before end, SSK, K1. 2 sts decreased.

(WS): P1, SSP, work in patterns as established to 3 sts before end, P2tog, P1. 2 sts decreased.

Work the decrease row every RS row 6 (6, 7, 8, 9, 10, 11, 12) times.

Rep the decrease row every 4th row 0 (0, 1, 1, 2, 2, 1, 1) times, then every row 17 (20, 18, 18, 16, 16, 18, 18) times.

Total 15 sts. BO 3 sts at the beginning of the next 2 rows. BO remaining 9 sts.

Finishing

Sew shoulder seams. Sew the neck extensions end to end then sew the selvedge edge to the bound off neck back easing to fit. Set in sleeves, easing the caps into place then sew side and sleeve seams. Sew on buttons.

Weave in ends. Wash and block garment to desired measurements.

詳細情報

Yarn

Sport weight yarn

約1200 (1300, 1350, 1400, 1500, 1600, 1700, 1800) yards, 1097 (1189, 1234, 1280, 1371, 1463, 1554, 1646) m

Berroco Corsica (90% Cotton, 10% Cashmere; 150 yards / 137 m, 50g)

8 (9, 9, 10, 10, 11, 12, 13)玉

サンプル色は 3619 Fig

Needles

1 x US3 (3.25 mm) 24" / 60 cm (またはそれ以上の長さ)の輪針か棒針

A US5 (3.75 mm) 24" / 60 cm (またはそれ以上の長さ) の輪針か棒針

または, ゲージに合わせた太さの針

Gauge (ブロッキング後)

US5 (3.75 mm)の針を使用し, メリヤス編みで24目 & 26段 = 10 cm

Sizes

出来上がり寸法: 胸囲XS (S, M, L, XL, 2XL, 3XL, 4XL) = 86.5 (91.5, 99, 106.5, 112, 119.5, 127, 132)cm

余裕: +5-10cm

モデルはSサイズを着用し, 余裕 として+5cm.

Tools

綴じ針, 段数マーカー (5), ボタン(1.80 mm x 5)

Skill Level

Note

前後身頃, 袖を別々に編んでから, 綴じるタイプのカーディガン.袖は往復編みで編んでから綴じ付ける.前立ては, ガーター編みで前身頃と一緒に編んでいく.

編みかた

後ろ身頃

小さい方の針を使用し, 指で掛ける作り目でCO101 (109, 117, 125, 133, 141, 149, 157)目.

セットアップ段 (WS): P1, *K1, P1; *からを最後まで繰り返す.

パターン通りに1目ゴム編みをあと28段編む.最後はWS.

大きい方の針に持ち替える.

模様編みセットアップ

段1 (RS): K1, *K1, YO, SSK, P1; *からを最後の4目前まで繰り返す, K1, YO, SSK, K1.

段2, 4, 6, 8 (WS): P4, *K1, P3; *からを最後の1目前まで繰り返す, P1.

段3: K1, *K1, K2tog, YO, P1; *からを最後の4目前まで繰り

返す, K1, K2tog, YO, K1.

段5: K1, *K2tog, YO, K1, P1; *からを最後の4目前まで繰り返す, K2tog, YO, K2.

段7: K1, *YO, SSK, K1, P1; *からを最後の4目前まで繰り返す, YO, SSK, K2.

COから46 cmになるまで, 段1-8を繰り返す.最後はWS.

袖ぐり

Note: 出来るだけ模様編みを続けるが, シェイピングにより, 次のYOや減目を編むことが出来ない場合は, メリヤス編みで編む.

次の2段の最初の6 (6, 7, 8, 9, 10, 11, 12)目をBO.

減目段(RS): K1, K2tog, 最後の3目前までパターン通りに編む , SSK, K1.2目減目.

全てのWS段: パターン通りに編む.

減目段を, 毎RS段であと5 (5, 6, 9, 10, 11, 12, 14)回繰り返す.

計 77 (85, 89, 89, 93, 97, 101, 103)目.

BO段から19.5 (20, 21, 21.5, 22, 23, 23, 23.5) cmになるまで, パターン通りに編む.

肩下がり

次の4段の最初の5 (6, 7, 7, 7, 8, 9, 9)目をBO, さらに次の2段の最初の4 (6, 6, 6, 8, 8, 8, 9)目をBO.計49目.

残りの目を全てBO, この部分が後ろ襟になる.

左前身頃

小さい方の針を使用し, 指で掛ける作り目でCO59 (63, 67, 71, 75, 79, 83, 87)目.

セットアップ段 (WS): K10 *P1, K1; *からを最後の1目前まで繰り返す, P1.

次の段: パターン通りに1目ゴム編みを最後の10目前まで編む, 最後までK.

パターン通りに, あと27段編む.最後はWS.

大きい方の針に持ち替える.

模様編みセットアップ

段1 (RS): K1, *P1, K1, YO, SSK; *からを最後の10目前まで繰り返す, K10.

段2, 4, 6, 8 (WS): K10, *P3, K1; *からを最後の1目前まで繰り返す, P1.

段3 (RS): K1, *P1, K1, K2tog, YO; *からを最後の10目前まで繰り返す, K10.

段5 (RS): K1, *P1, K2tog, YO, K1; *からを最後の10目前まで繰り返す, K10.

段7 (RS): K1, *P1, YO, SSK, K1; *からを最後の10目前まで繰り返す, K10.

COから41 cmになるまで, 段1-8を繰り返す.最後はWS.

襟ぐり

減目段(RS): 最後の11目前までパターン通りに編む, K2tog, K9. 1目減目.

全てのWS段: K10, 最後までパターン通りに編む.

減目段を次のRSで２回, [4段目で１回, 次のRS段で１回], [ ]をあと9回編む.

同時に, 身頃が46 cmになりWSを編んだ後, 次の段の最初の6 (6, 7, 8, 9, 10, 11, 12)目をBO.

WSを1段編む.

袖ぐり

減目段(RS): K1, K2tog, 最後までパターン通りに編む.1目減目.

毎RS段ごとに 減目段をあと5 (5, 6, 9, 10, 11, 12, 14)回繰り返す.

計24 (28, 30, 30, 32, 34, 36, 37)目.

BO段から19.5 (20, 21, 21.5, 22, 23, 23, 23.5)cmになるまで, パターン通りに編む.最後はWS.

肩下がり

次のRSで２回, 最初の5 (6, 7, 7, 7, 8, 9, 9)目をBO, さらに次のRSの最初の4 (6, 6, 6, 8, 8, 8, 9)目をBO.計10目.

後ろ襟

次の段(WS): K10, 巻き増し目でCO1目(端目となる).計11目.

ガーター編みを30段編む.全ての目をBO.

ここで, ボタンの位置を決める.

COから5cm(19段目)と, 襟ぐりの減らし始めに段数マーカーを付ける.

その間を均等に４分割してそれぞれ段数マーカーを付ける.

このボタンの位置に対応させて, 右前身頃にボタンホールを作る.

右前身頃

小さい方の針を使用し, 指で掛ける作り目でCO 59 (63, 67, 71, 75, 79, 83, 87)目.

セットアップ段 (WS): *P1, K1; *からを最後の11目前まで繰り返す, P1, K10.

次の段: K10, パターン通りに1目ゴム編みを最後まで編む.

COから5 cm(18段目)になるまでパターン通り編む.最後はWS.

次の段(ボタンホール段): K4, K2tog, YO, 最後までパターン通りに編む.

Note: 以下, 左前身頃で設定したボタン位置の段に来たら, ボタンホール段を編むようにする.

同時に, パターン通りにあと11段編む.最後はWS.

大きい方の針に持ち替える.

模様編みセットアップ

段1 (RS): K10, *K1, YO, SSK, P1; *からを最後の1目前まで繰り返す, K1.

段2, 4, 6, 8 (WS): P1, *K1, P3; *からを最後の10目前まで繰り返す, K10.

段3: K10, *K1, K2tog, YO, P1; *からを最後の1目前まで繰り返す, K1.

段5: K10, *K2tog, YO, K1, P1; *からを最後の1目前まで繰り返す, K1.

段7: K10, *YO, SSK, K1, P1; *からを最後の1目前まで繰り返す, K1.

COから41 cmになるまで, 段1-8を繰り返す.最後はWS.

襟ぐり

減目段(RS): K9, SSK, 最後までパターン通りに編む.1目減目.

全てのWS段: 最後の10目前までパターン通りに編む, K10.

減目段を次のRSで２回, [4段目で１回, 次のRS段で１回], [ ] をあと9回編む.

同時に, 身頃が後ろ身頃と同じ長さになりRSを編んだ後, 次の段の最初6 (6, 7, 8, 9, 10, 11, 12)目をBO.

減目段 (RS): 最後の3目前までパターン通りに編む, SSK, K1.1目減目.

減目段を毎RS段であと5 (5, 6, 9, 10, 11, 12, 14)回繰り返す.

計 24 (28, 30, 30, 32, 34, 36, 37)目.

BO段から19.5 (20, 21, 21.5, 22, 23, 23, 23.5)cmになるまで, パターン通りに編む.最後はRS.

肩下がり

次のWSで２回, 最初の5 (6, 7, 7, 7, 8, 9, 9)目をBO, さらに次のWSの最初の4 (6, 6, 6, 8, 8, 8, 9)目をBO.計10目.

後ろ襟

次の段(RS): K10, 巻き増目でCO1目(端目となる).計11目.

ガーター編みを29段編む.全ての目をBO.

袖(左右同様)

小さい方の針を使用し, 指で掛ける作り目でCO 49 (49, 53, 57, 57, 61, 65, 69)目.

セットアップ段(WS): *P1, K1; *からを最後の1目前まで繰り返す, P1.

パターン通りに1目ゴム編みをあと22段編む.最後はWS.

大きい方の針に持ち替える.

模様編みセットアップ

段1 (RS): K1, *K1, YO, SSK, P1; *からを最後の4目前まで繰り返す, K1, YO, SSK, K1.

段2, 4, 6, 8 (WS): P4, *K1, P3; *からを最後の1目前まで繰り返す, P1.

段3: K1, *K1, K2tog, YO, P1; *からを最後の4目前まで繰り返す, K1, K2tog, YO, K1.

段5: K1, *K2tog, YO, K1, P1; *からを最後の4目前まで繰り返す, K2tog, YO, K2.

段7: K1, *YO, SSK, K1, P1; *からを最後の4目前まで繰り返す, YO, SSK, K2.

増目段: K1, M1, 最後の1目前までパターン通りに編む, M1, K1.2目増目.

増目段を8 (6, 6, 6, 6, 6, 8) 段毎に, あと11 (14, 13, 13, 14, 14, 15, 15)回編む. 計73 (79, 81, 85, 87, 91, 97, 101)目.

COから49 cmになるまで, パターン通りに編む.最後はWS.

袖山

次の2段の最初の6 (6, 7, 8, 9, 10, 11, 12)目をBO.

減目段の編み方は下記の通り:

(RS): K1, K2tog, 最後の3目前までパターン通り編む, SSK, K1.2目減目.

(WS): P1, SSP, 最後の3目前までパターン通り編む, P2tog, P1.2目減目.

特に指定がない場合は, パターン通りに編む.

RS段の減目段を, 6 (6, 7, 8, 9, 10, 11, 12)回編む.

減目段を4段毎に0 (0, 1, 1, 2, 2, 1, 1)回, さらに減目段を毎段17 (20, 18, 18, 16, 16, 18, 18)回編む.計15目.

次の2段の最初の3目をBO.残りの9目をBO.

仕上げ

両肩をはぎあわせる. 左右前身頃の後ろ襟をつなげ, 端目を後ろ身頃に綴じつける.袖山を袖ぐりに合わせて身頃に綴じつけ, それから前後身頃の脇とそで下をはぎ合わせる. ボタンをボタンホール位置に合うように縫い付ける.

糸始末をする.優しく洗って好みの長さにブロッキングする.

Nadeshiko by Leila Raabe

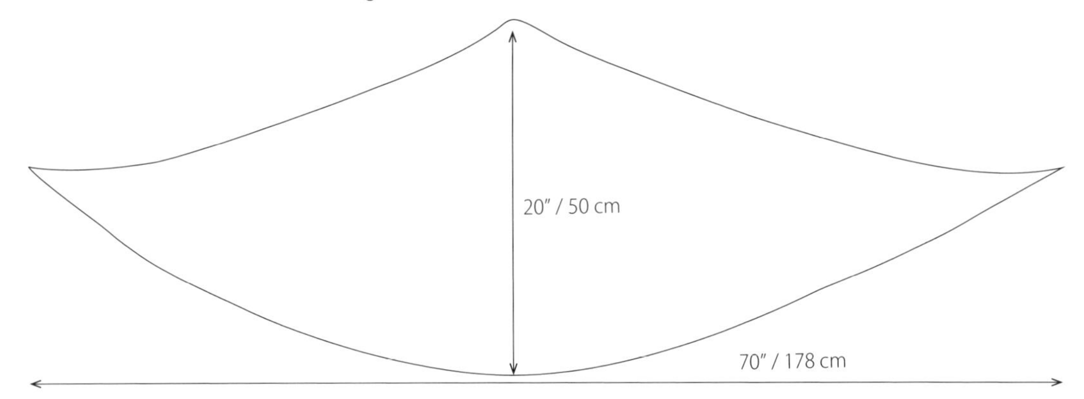

Specifications

Yarn

Heavy lace weight yarn, approximately 540 yards / 495 m

2 skeins of Quince & Co. Piper (50 % Texas super kid mohair / 50 % Texas superfine merino; 305 yards / 50g).

Sample shown in Odessa

Needle

A US 4 (3.5 mm) 24" / 60 cm (or longer) circular needle or needle to obtain gauge

Gauge (after blocking)

22 sts and 32 rows = 4" / 10 cm in St st

Gauge is not crucial, but final dimensions and yardage used will be affected if gauge differs from above

Size

70" / 178 cm wingspan x 20" / 50 cm depth at center

Tools

Stitch markers (10), tapestry needle, T-pins, blocking wires (optional)

Skill Level

Notes

- Shawl begins with a cast on of 4 sts and shaped outward with increases - first the half-pi method, transitioning into double increases at the two side edges every RS row (with Kfb increases during the textured knit-purl section, double-yarnover increases during the lace sections).
- Additional shaping increases occur at various sections; with the exception of these areas, stitch count will grow at a rate of 4 sts every other row.
- Shawl edges are comprised of St st for the first 3 and last 3 sts of each row, outside of the shawl increases.

Instructions

CO 4 sts using the long tail cast on.

Stockinette Tab

Beginning with WS, work in St st for 8 rows. At end of 8th row (RS), do not turn.

Rotate work and from side edge, pick up and knit 4 sts along side edge, turn and pick up 2 sts from CO edge. Total 10 sts.

Next Row (WS): P all sts.

Begin Half-Pi Shaping

Next Row (RS): K3, (YO, K1) 4 times, YO, K3. 5 sts increased, total 15 sts.

Next Row (WS): P all sts.

Work 4 rows even in St st.

Increase Row (RS): K3, *YO, K1; repeat from * to last 3 sts, YO, K3. 10 sts increased, total 25 sts.

Next Row (WS): P all sts.

Texture Pattern:

Work 4 rows even (no increasing) in following pattern:

Row 1 (RS): K all sts.

Row 2 (WS): P3, (K1, P1) to last 4 sts, K1, P3.

Row 3: K all sts.

Row 4: P all sts.

Repeat last 4 rows once more.

Next Row (RS): Work Increase Row. 20 sts increased, total 45 sts.

Next Row (WS): P all sts.

Repeat rows 1–4 of Texture Pattern 4 more times.

Next Row (RS): Work Increase Row. 40 sts increased, total 85 sts.

Next Row (WS): P all sts.

Work in St st for 5 rows.

Next row (WS): P3, *K1, P1; repeat from * to last 4 sts, K1, P3.

Total 85 sts: 3 edge sts, 79 main sts, 3 edge sts.

Begin Crescent Shaping

Half-pi shaping ends at this point and crescent shaping begins by way of double increases at the beginning and end of every RS row.

Shape Crescent

Rows 1, 3, and 5 (RS): K2, (Kfb) twice, K to last 5 sts, (Kfb) twice, K3. 4 sts increased.

Row 2 and 4 (WS): P all sts.

Row 6 (WS): P3, *K1, P1; repeat from * to last 4 sts, K1, P3.

Repeat last 6 rows once more: total 109 sts.

Shape Shawl Body

Next row (RS): K2, (Kfb) twice, K17, Kfb, K21 Kfb, K22, Kfb, K21, Kfb, K to last 5 sts, (Kfb) twice, K3. 8 sts increased, total 117 sts.

Next row (WS): P all sts.

Work rows 1–6 of Shape Crescent section above, then work Rows 1 and 2 once more.

Work rows 1–6 of Shape Crescent section above once more.

28 sts increased, total 145 sts (3 edge sts, 139 main sts, 3 sts).

Next row (RS): K2, (Kfb) twice, K43, Kfb, K47, Kfb, K to last 5 sts, (Kfb) twice, K3. 6 sts increased, total 151 sts.

Next row (WS): P all sts.

Next row: K2, (Kfb) twice, K to last 5 sts, (Kfb) twice, K3. 4 sts increased, total 155 sts.

Repeat last 2 rows once more. 4 sts increased, 159 sts.

Next row (WS): P all sts.

Begin Lace Section

From this section on, double-YO increases will be worked in place of the two (Kfb) increases that shape each edge of the shawl to this point.

Begin Chart 1:

Work Chart 1 twice.

You will be repeating in the bracket for 19 times at first time, and 21 times for 2nd time.32 sts increased, 191 sts.

Begin Chart 2:

Note: It's a "half-drop" version of the pattern in chart 1. In chart 1 this motif is aligned vertically so that the same stitches stack on top of each other in successive rows. In the next section, the same stitch pattern is used, but shifts over by 4 stitches every 4 rows.

Work Chart 2, 7 times.

You will be repeating in the bracket for 23 times at first time, then add one more repeat every time you complete rows 1- 4 of the chart.

56 sts increased, total 247 sts.

Begin Chart 3A:

Work Chart 3A once.

You will be repeating in the bracket for 15 times.

16 sts increased, total 263 sts.

Begin Chart 3B:

Work Chart 3B 3 times.

You will be repeating in the bracket for 16 times at first time, then add one more repeat every time you complete rows 1- 8 of the chart.

On the final row of the last repeat, PM on either side of center stitch (stitch 156). 16 sts increased each time. 48 sts increased, total 311 sts.

Begin Chart 4A:

In this section new shaping begins with a YO at either side of the central stitch and will continue to grow by 2 stitches throughout the remainder of the charted sections, while the shawl edges also continue to increase with the 2 YOs at each side edge as established.

The dashed lines on this chart denote marker placement.

Work Chart 4A once.

You will be repeating in the both brackets for 9 times.

24 sts increased, total 335 sts,

Begin Chart 4B:

Work Chart 4B once.

You will be repeating in the both brackets for 10 times.

On the final row, PM for next section: one at either side of the 76th st and 124th st in from each edge of the shawl (8 stitch markers total placed around 4 stitches, two markers each). 24 sts increased, total 359 sts.

Begin Chart 4C:

In this final section 4 new shaping points (2 on each half of the shawl) occur at the marked stitches similar to the shaping that occurred in Chart 4A.

The charts have been both split into sections, and the 16-stitch rep compressed to a single column (shown shaded grey with a thick outline). Begin with "Chart 4C - to center section", then continue to "Chart 4C continued - second half" for the rest of the row.

When you come to a grey column, work the number of 16-st rep as instructed.

The dashed lines on this chart denote marker placement from the final row of the previous section.

Work rows 1–8 of Chart 4C once. 56 sts increased, 415 sts.

Next row (RS): Next row (RS): K3, (YO) twice, K2, *K1,

YO, Sk2p, YO; repeat from * to last 6 sts (RM all as encountered), K3, (YO) twice, K3. 4 sts increased, 419 sts.

Next row (WS): P4, P tbl, P to last 4 sts, P tbl, P3.

(RS): K1, *slip st just worked from RH needle back to LH needle and knit together with next st on needle; repeat from * to end, BO all sts.

Finishing

Wet block and pin shawl to schematic measurements using blocking wires and / or T-pins, allowing to dry completely before unpinning.

- ☐ K on RS, P on WS / RSでK、WSでP
- ⊡ P on RS / RSでP
- ○ YO / 掛け目
- K2tog / 左上2目1度
- SSK / 右上2目1度
- SK2P / 右上3目1度
- △ S2KP / 中上3目1度
- ⋮ Denotes stitch marker placement 点線　マーカーの位置
- ❙ Denotes bracketed stitch repeat 繰り返し位置

Chart 1
work row 1-8 twice　段1 - 8を2回編む

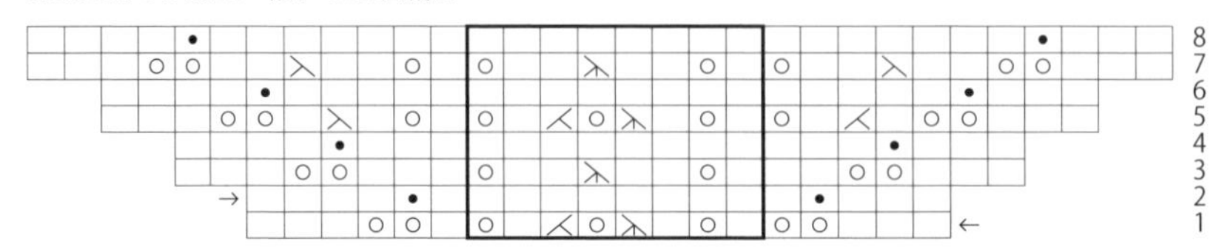

Chart 2
work row 1-4 seven times　段1 - 4を7回編む

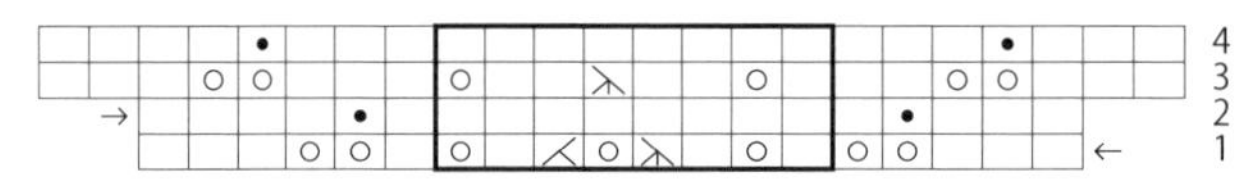

Chart 3A
work row 1-8 once　段1 - 8を1回編む

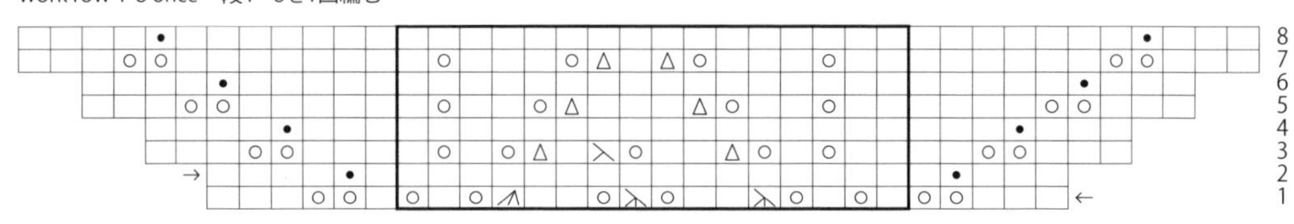

Chart 3B
work row 1-8 three times　段1 - 8を3回編む

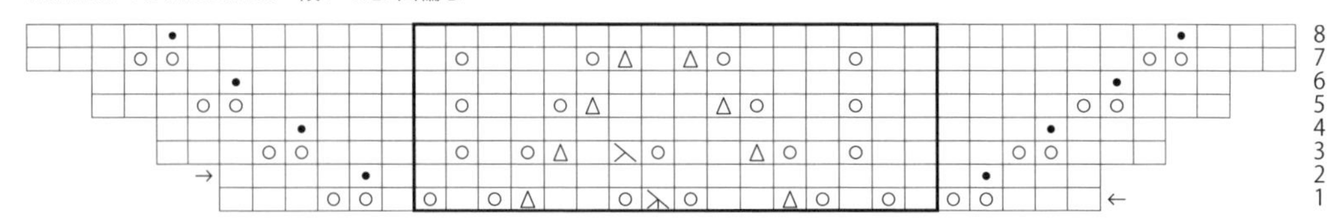

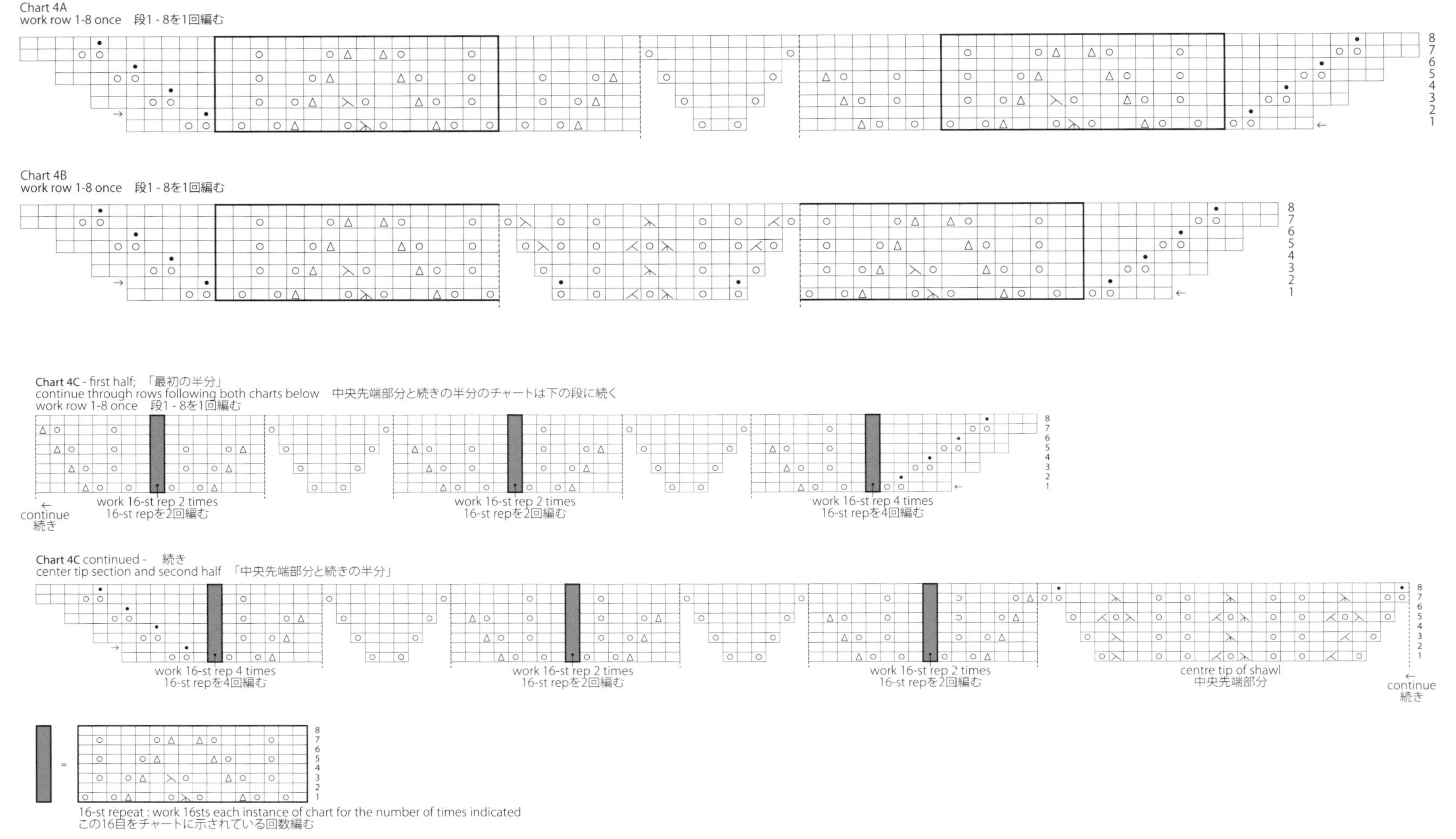
Chart 4A
work row 1-8 once　段1 - 8を1回編む
Chart 4B
work row 1-8 once　段1 - 8を1回編む
Chart 4C - first half; 「最初の半分」
continue through rows following both charts below　中央先端部分と続きの半分のチャートは下の段に続く
work row 1-8 once　段1 - 8を1回編む
continue
続き
work 16-st rep 2 times
16-st repを2回編む
work 16-st rep 2 times
16-st repを2回編む
work 16-st rep 4 times
16-st repを4回編む
Chart 4C continued -　続き
center tip section and second half　「中央先端部分と続きの半分」
work 16-st rep 4 times
16-st repを4回編む
work 16-st rep 2 times
16-st repを2回編む
work 16-st rep 2 times
16-st repを2回編む
centre tip of shawl
中央先端部分
continue
続き
16-st repeat : work 16sts each instance of chart for the number of times indicated
この16目をチャートに示されている回数編む

詳細情報

Yarn

Heavy lace weight yarn

約540ヤード, 495m

Quince & Co. Piper (50 % Texas super kid mohair / 50 % Texas superfine merino; 305 yards / 280m, 50g) 2かせ

サンプル色は, Odessa

Needle

1 × US 4 (3.5 mm) 24″ / 60 cm (または, それ以上の長さ)の輪針

または, ゲージに合わせた太さの針

Gauge (ブロッキング後)

メリヤス編みで22目 & 32段 = 10 cm

ゲージは重要ではないが, もしもゲージが上記と違う場合, 出来上がり寸法と糸量はそれに伴って変わってくる.

Size

出来上がり寸法; 幅178 cm x 高さ 50 cm

Tools

目数マーカー (10), 綴じ針, Tピン, ブロッキングワイヤー (オプション)

Skill Level

Notes

・ショールは4目の作り目で始まり, 外側に向かって, 毎RS段の両端でそれぞれ2目(テクスチャーパターン部分でKfbの増目, レース模様部分で2目の掛け目) の増目で半月型(はじめの半分)に広がっていく.

・いくつかのセクションでの追加の増目は, 例外の箇所を除き, 目数は1段おきに4目ずつ増えていく.

・ショールの端は, 増目部分の外側で最初3目, 最後3目をメリヤス編みで編んでいく.

編みかた

指で掛ける作り目でCO 4.

タブを作る

編み始めをWSとし, メリヤス編みで8段編む.8段目はRS, 編地を返さない.

編地を回転させて, サイドから4目拾う, さらに回転させてCO段から2目拾う.計10目.

次の段(WS): 全ての目をP.

半月型の開始

次の段(RS): K3, (YO, K1)を4回編む, YO, K3. 5目増目, 計15目.

次の段(WS): 全てP.

メリヤス編みで4段編む.

増目段(RS): K3, *YO, K1, *からを最後から3目前まで繰り返す, YO, K3.10目増目, 計25目.

次の段(WS): 全てP.

テクスチャーパターン

次のように4段編む(増目は無し):

段1(RS): 全てK.

段2(WS): P3, (K1, P1)を最後から4目前まで繰り返す, K1, P3.

段3: 全てK.

段4: 全てP.

最後の4段をあと1回編む.

次の段(RS): 増目段を編む. 20目増目, 計45目.

次の段(WS): 全てP.

テクスチャーパターンの1-4段をあと4回編む.

次の段(RS): 増目段を編む. 40目増目, 計85目.

次の段(WS): 全てP.

メリヤス編みで5段編む.

次の段(WS): P3, *K1, P1, *からを最後から4目前まで繰り返す, K1, P3.

計85目 (端目3目, 本体79目, 端目3目).

三日月型の開始

ここまでで半月型が終わり, 毎RS段の最初と最後の2目増目をしながら三日月型に編む.

三日月型の形成

段1, 3と5(RS): K2, Kfbを2回編む, 最後から5目前までK, Kfbを2回編む, K3. 4目増目.

段2と4(WS): 全てP.

段6(WS): P3, *K1, P1, *からを最後から4目前まで繰り返す, K1, P3.

最後の6段をあと1回編む.計109目.

ショール本体の形成

次の段(RS): K2, Kfbを2回編む, K17, Kfb, K21, Kfb, K22, Kfb, K21, Kfb, 最後の5目前までK, Kfbを2回編む, K3. 8目増目, 計117目.

次の段(WS): 全てP.

三日月型形成セクションの段1–6を編む, 続けて段1, 2を1回編む.

三日月型形成セクションの段1–6を1回編む.

28目増目, 計145目 (端目3目, 本体139目, 端目3目).

次の段(RS): K2, Kfbを2回編む, K43, Kfb, K47, Kfb, 最後から5目前まで, Kfbを2回編む, K3.6目増目, 計151目.

次の段(WS): 全てP.

次の段: K2, Kfbを2回編む, 最後から5目前までK, Kfbを2回編む, K3. 4目増目, 計155目.

最後の2段をあと1回編む.

4目増目, 計159目.

次の段(WS): 全てP.

レース模様の開始

このセクションから, ここまでショールの両端で行っていた2目のKfbを使った増目が, 掛け目2目になる.

Chart 1の開始:

Chart 1を2回編む.

１回目は繰り返し部分を19回編み, 2回目は21回編む.

32目増目, 計191目.

Chart 2の開始:

Chart 2を7回編む.

1回目は繰り返し部分を23回編み, その後Chart の段1 - 4が終わる度に繰り返し部分を1回増やして編んでいく.

56目増目, 計247目.

Chart 3Aの開始:

Chart 3Aを1回編む. 繰り返し部分は15回編む.

16目増目, 計263目.

Chart 3Bの開始:

Chart 3Bを3回編む.

1回目は繰り返し部分を16回編み, その後Chart の段1 - 8が完了する度に繰り返し部分を1回増やして編んでいく.

最後の段で中心の目(156番目の目)の両側にPM.

両側で各16目増目. 48目増目, 計311目.

Chart 4Aの開始:

このセクションでは中心の目の両側に入れたマーカー間で2目増目をし、両端の2目のYOによる増目も続ける。

Chart の点線は, マーカーを入れる箇所を表している.

Chart 4Aを1回編む. 両側の繰り返し部分は各9回編む.

24目増目, 計335目.

Chart 4Bの開始:

Chart 4Bを1回編む. 両側の繰り返し部分はそれぞれ10回編む.

最後の段で次のセクションのためにMをショールの両端からそれぞれ76番目と124番目の目の両側に入れる(4目の両側にそれぞれ2個ずつの合計8個のマーカーを入れる).

24目増目, 計359目.

Chart 4Cの開始:

この最後のセクションでは, Chart 4Aで出てきた増目と同じように, 4つの新しい増目ポイント(ショールの半分に2カ所)がマーカー間で行われる.

Chart は中央部分から左右2つのセクションに分かれていく。Chart の見かたとしては「最初の半分」を編み, 次に「中央先端部分と続きの半分」を編む.

グレーの部分にきたら, 16-st repを指定された回数編む.

Chart の点線は前段の最後の段で入れたマーカーの位置を表している .

Chart 4Cの段1－8を1回編む.

56目増目, 計415目.

次の段(RS): K3, YOを2回編む, K1, *K1, YO, Sk2p, YO, *からを最後から5目前まで編む(全てのマーカーをRM), K2tog, YOを2回編む, K3.4目増目, 計419目.

次の段(WS): P4, P tbl, 最後から4目前までP, P tbl, P3.

次の段(RS): K1, *編んだ目を右針から左針に滑らせて, 次の目と一緒にK2tog, *からを最後まで編む, 全ての目をBO.

仕上げ

濡らしてブロッキングする, ブロッキングワイヤーかTピンでスキーム通りにショールをピン打ちする, 完全に乾いてからピンを外すようにする.

Sumire by Nadia Crétin-Léchenne

Specifications

Yarn

Fingering weight yarn

(MC) Approximately 410 yards, 375m

(CC) Approximately 100 yards, 91 m

Madelinetosh Tosh Merino Light (100 % Merino; 420 yards / 384 m)

Madelinetosh Unicorn Tail (100% Merino; 52 yards / 48 m)

Sample shown in Moonstone (MC) 1 skein, Antler (CC) 2 skeins

Needle

A US 6 (4.00 mm) 32" / 80 cm circular needle

or needle to obtain gauge

Gauge (after blocking)

18 stitches & 24 rows = 4" / 10 cm in Lace pattern with US 6 (4.0 mm) needle

Size

58" / 148 cm wingspan and 24" / 62 cm height

Tools

Stitch markers (4), tapestry needle

Skill Level

Stitch Guide

Sk2p

Sl1, K2tog, pass slipped stitch over (double decrease)

Picot bind off

BO 6 sts, *place the last st on the right needle to left needle, CO 2 sts using cable cast on, BO 9 sts; rep from * to 5 sts before M (without the st on the right needle). Place the last st on the right needle to left needle, CO 2 sts, BO 12 sts.

*Place the last st on the right needle to left needle, CO 2 sts, BO 9 sts; rep from * to 4 sts before M (without the st on the right needle). Place the last st on the right needle to left needle, CO 2 sts and BO to end of row.

Note

It is a triangular shawl, knitted in one piece from the top down.

The lace pattern is worked with MC, then garter stitch border is worked with CC. Finishing with picot bind off.

Instructions

Garter-tab cast on

With MC, CO 3 sts using long tail cast on. K 10 rows, always slipping the first st of each row. Rotate work 90 ° clockwise, pick up and knit 5 sts along the side. Rotate work again 90° , pick up and knit 3 sts along the cast on edge. (11 sts)

Set up row : Sl1, K2, PM, P2, PM, P1, PM, P2, PM, K3.

Row 1 (RS) : Sl1, K2, SM, YO, K to M, YO, SM, K1, SM, YO, K to M, YO, SM, K3.

Row 2 (WS) : Sl1, K2, SM, YO, P to last M, YO, SM, K3.

Work rows 1-2 once more. (23 sts)

Lace part

You are going to start the lace pattern, while still increasing 4 sts on each RS row, and 2 sts on each WS row. The lace chart present only the RS rows and doesn't show the edge stitches and the central stitch.

Follow the lace chart for RS rows: Work the edge stitches (Sl1, K2), chart A, central stitch (K1), chart B, the edge stitches (K3).

All WS rows : Sl1, K2, SM, YO, work sts as they come to the last M (P the YO), YO, SM, K3.

Work rows 1-16 of the lace pattern 6 times total, then work rows 1-8 once. 335 sts.

Edging

Cut MC and continue with CC.

Row 1 (RS) : Sl1, K2, SM, YO, K toM, YO, SM, K1, SM, YO, K toM, YO, SM, K3.

Row 2 (WS) : Sl1, K2, SM, YO, K to last M, YO, SM, K3.

Work rows 1-2 of the edging 5 more times. (371 sts)

Next row (RS): work picot binding off.

Finishing

Weave in all ends.

Soak your project in a large quantity of lukewarm water, for at least 30 minutes.

Squeeze it gently – without twisting ! – between towels to pull out as much water as you can.

Put the shawl in place on a dry, flat surface, pinning out the picots.

Let it dry.

詳細情報

Yarn

Fingering weight yarn

(MC) 約410ヤード, 375m

(CC) 約100ヤード, 91m

Madelinetosh Tosh Merino Light (100% Merino; 420ヤード/ 384m)

Madelinetosh Unicorn Tail (100% Merino; 52ヤード/ 48m)

サンプル色はMoonstone (MC)1カセ, Antler (CC)2カセ

Needles

1 x US 6 (4.00mm) 32" / 80cm(またはより長い)の輪針

または, ゲージに合わせた太さの針

Gauge (ブロッキング後)

US 6 (4.0mm)の針を使用し, レース模様で18目 & 24段 = 10cm

Sizes

出来上がり寸法; 幅148cm x 高さ62cm

Tools

目数マーカー (4), 綴じ針

Skill Level

Stitch Guide

Picot bind off

BO6, *最後の目を左針から右針に移す, Cable cast onでCO2, BO9, *からをMの5目前まで(右針に移した目は除く)繰り返す, 右針の目を左針に移す, Cable cast onでCO2, BO12, *最後の目を左針から右針に移す, Cable cast onでCO2, BO9, *からをマーカーの4目前まで(右針に移した目は除く)繰り返す, 右針の目を左針に移す, Cable cast onでCO2, 最後までBO.

Note

トップダウンの三角形のショール.レース模様を編んだ後, 色を変えてガーター部分を編み, 最後はピコットBOで終わる.

編みかた

Garter-tab cast on

MCで, 指で掛ける作り目でCO3.最初の目はすべり目して, 10段K.編み地を90°時計回りに回転する.脇から5目拾い目.編み地を90°時計回りに回転する.編み始めの目から3目拾い目.〈計10目〉

セットアップ段: Sl1, K2, PM, P2, PM, P1, PM, P2, PM, K3.

段1(RS): Sl1, K2, SM, YO, MまでK, YO, SM, K1, SM, YO, MまでK, YO, SM, K3.

段2(WS): Sl1, K2, SM, YO, 最後のMまでP, YO, SM, K3.

段1, 2をあと1回編む.〈計23目〉

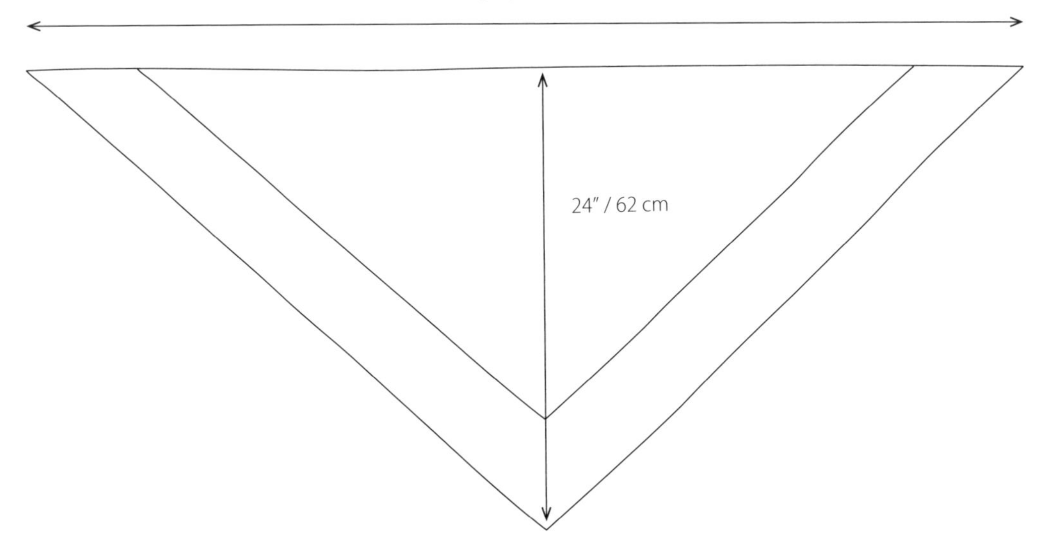

レース模様

ここからはRSで4目, WSで2目増目しながら, レース模様を編む.チャートを参考にする.レースチャートはRS段のみを表しており, エッジ部分と中央の目はチャートに記載されていない.

RS段: エッジ部分として (Sl1, K2), チャートA, 中央の目(K1), チャートB, 最後にエッジ部分(K3).

全てのWS段: Sl1, K2, SM, YO, パターン通りに最後のMまで編む(YOはP), YO, SM, K3.

段1-16のレース模様を計6回編む.さらに段1-8を1回編む.計335目.

縁編み

MCを切り, CCで編み始める.

段1(RS): Sl1, K2, SM, YO, MまでK, YO, SM, K1, SM, YO, MまでK, YO, SM, K3.

段2(WS): Sl1, K2, SM, YO, 最後のMまでK, YO, SM, K3.

段1-2をあと5回繰り返す.計371目.

次の段(RS): picot bind offでBO.

仕上げ

糸始末する.

多めのぬるま湯に出来上がった作品を最低30分浸す.捻らないように, 優しく水を絞る.タオルの間に挟んで出来るだけ水を絞る.平坦なところで乾かす.ピコットのところはピンで留める.

- □ RS: K, WS: P
- ● RS: P, WS: K
- ○ YO
- ／ K2tog
- ＼ SSK
- 木 Sk2p
- ■ No stitch (目がない)
- Repeat

Chart A (right side) / チャートA (右側)

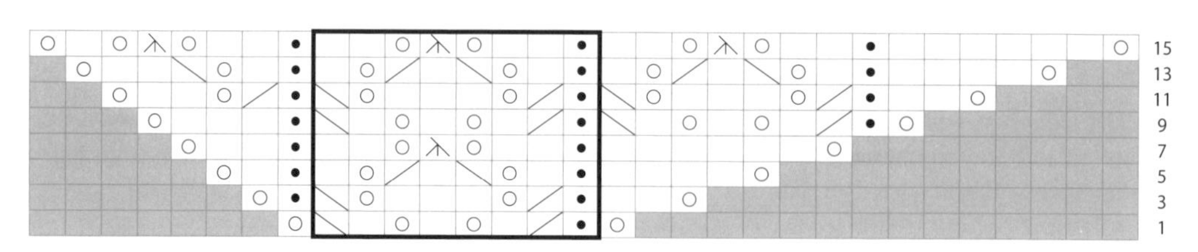

Chart B (left side) / チャートB (左側)

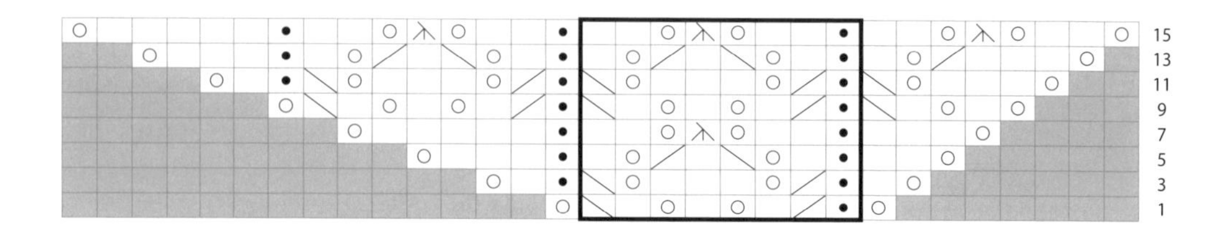

Abbreviations / Pattern Notes

K	Knit	表目
P	Purl	裏目
K tbl	Knit through back of loop	表のねじり目
RS	Right Side	表面
WS	Wrong Side	裏面
CO	Cast On	作り目
BO	Bind Off	伏せ目
BOR	Beginning of round	段の開始位置
M	Marker	マーカー
PM	Place Marker	マーカーを入れる
SM	Slip Marker	マーカーを移す
RM	Remove Marker	マーカーを外す
St st	Stockinette stitch	メリヤス編み
TW	Turn work	編地を裏返す
RH	Right Hand	右手
LH	Left Hand	左手
st(s)	Stitch(es)	編み目
DPN	Double pointed needles	4本棒針
rep	Repeat	繰り返す
psso	Pass slipped stitch over	すべらせた目に被せる
Sl wyb	Slip st with yarn in back	すべり目
Sl wyf	Slip st with yarn in front	浮き目
YO	Yarn over	掛け目
Kfb	Knit into front & back of st	目の手前と後ろのループに編み入れる(1目増)

K2tog	Knit 2 together	左上2目一度
K2tog tbl	Knit 2 together through the back loop	左上2目一度(ねじり目)
K1B **K1 below**	Insert right needle into st below the next one on left hand needle, wrap yarn and pull through, slip both sts off needle	引き上げ目
Skp	Slip one stitch knitwise, then knit the next stitch. Pass the slipped stitch over the knit stitch and off the right needle.	右上2目一度
SSK	Slip 2 sts as if to knit, knit them together thru the back loops	右上2目一度
P2tog	Purl 2 sts together	裏左上2目一度
P2tog tbl	Insert the right needle into the back loops of two sts at once and purl	裏左上2目一度(ねじり目)
SSP	Slip 2 stitches as if to K. Slip the two slipped stitches back to the left needle. Then purl them together through the back loops.	裏右上2目一度
SSSK	Slip slip slip knit (double decrease)	右上3目一度
S2kp	Slip 2, knit 1 pass slipped sts over	右上3目一度
Sk2p	Slip, k2tog, psso	中上3目一度
K3tog	Knit 3 together	左上3目一度
rep	repeat	繰り返し

Cable cast on

Begin with a slipknot and one knitted cast on stitch if there are no established stitches. Insert right needle between first two stitches on left needle. Wrap yarn as if knit, draw yarn through to complete stitch and slip this new stitch to left needle.

Backward loop cast on

Start with a slip knot on the needle in your right hand. Grab your yarn with your left hand and stretch it out a few inches from your needle. Take your index finger and wrap the yarn around it. Begin by going over the top, to under, and then around to the top again. You should now have a loop on your finger. Slide your knitting needle into the side of the loop, next to your finger. Pull your finger out and tighten the loop on the needle. Repeat until you have desired number of stitches.

Knitted cast on

Start with a slip knot on the needle in your left hand.

Insert the right needle into the slip knot and work a knit

Cable cast on

まず左針1目を作り、その目を表編みする。右針に掛かった目を左針で目の後ろ側から針を入れ、左針に移す。これで左針に2目が掛かった状態。

＊次に左針の先頭にある2目の間に表編みするように針を入れ、右針に目を作る。先ほどと同じように、右針に掛かった目を左針で目の後ろ側から針を入れ、左針に移す。＊

＊～＊部分を必要な目数になるまで繰り返す。

Knitted cast on

まず左針1目を作り、その目を落とさないようにしながら表編みを編むように糸を引き出す。右針を傾けるようにねじって左針に目をかける。これで左針に2目がかかった状態。これを必要な目数になるまで繰り返す。

Long tail tubular CO (一目ゴム編みの作り目)

出来上がり幅の3倍の長さの糸を残して、引き結びで１目作り、編み針に置く(この目を１目と数える)。指で掛ける作り目と同様に針を右手に持ち、糸端を向こう、糸玉

stitch, but do NOT slip it off of the left needle. Tilt the right needle to the right and insert the left needle into the loop you've pulled up. You are now in position to complete another knit stitch. Repeat the instructions.

Crochet Provisional Cast On

Make a slip knot loop and place it on the crochet hook. Holding knitting needle in your left hand, *bring yarn over needle from behind, then over crochet hook and draw through loop on hook. Bring yarn to back between hook and needle. 1 st cast on. Rep from * until you have the required number of sts less 1. For final st, transfer the loop on crochet hook to the needle.

Garter Stitch Row 1: Purl. Row 2: Knit.

M1L, M1 (M1PL)
Insert left needle, from front to back, under strand of yarn which runs between next stitch on left needle and last stitch on right needle; knit (purl) this stitch through back loop. 1 stitch increased.

M1R (M1PR)
Insert left needle, from back to front, under strand of yarn which runs between next stitch on left needle and last stitch on right needle; knit (purl) this stitch through front loop. 1 stitch increased.

Magic loop
Bend the cable of your circular needle so the stitches are divided in half. Slide the stitches back onto the needles. With the needle tips pointing right and parallel, pull on the back needle and draw up enough slack on the cable to allow you to use that needle tip to work the stitches on the front needle. Knit all of the stitches on the front needle and continue around.

W&T (Wrap & Turn)
To w&t on a RS row, knit to point specified in pattern, bring yarn to front of work between needles, slip next stitch to right-hand needle, bring yarn around this stitch to back of work, slip stitch back to left-hand needle, turn work to begin purling back in the other direction.

To w&t on a WS row, purl to point specified in pattern, bring yarn to back of work between needles, slip next stitch to right-hand needle, bring yarn around this stitch to front of work, slip stitch back to left-hand needle, turn work to begin knitting back in the other direction.

Working Wraps Together with Wrapped Stitches:

When working a RS row: Knit to wrapped stitch. Slip next stitch from left needle to right needle, use tip of left

を手前にし、人差し指と親指に糸を掛ける 。

ステップ1: 針先を2本の糸の後ろ側から下へ持ってくる。親指側の糸にループを1つ作るように2本の糸の間を前から後ろに引っ掛けて、2本の糸の後ろ側から持ち上げる(裏目の作り目１目)。

ステップ2: 針先を親指の下から入れて、1ループを作るように2本の糸の間から人差し指の方の糸を前から後ろに向かって糸を掛け、両方の糸の後ろ側から前に持ってくる(表目の作り目1目)。

ステップ１と 2を必要な目数になるまで繰り返す。

ガーター編み 段1: 全てP。段2: 全てK。

M1L 、M1 (M1PL) 1目増目:

目と目の間に渡っている糸を左針で手前側からすくう。このすくった目をねじり表編み(裏編み)する。

M1R (M1PR) 1目増目:

目と目の間に渡っている糸を左針で後ろ側からすくう。この目をねじり表編み(裏編み)する。この時、目の向きが通常と異なっているため、針は手前から差し込む。

W&T (Wrap & Turn)

表側でのW&T: パターン内でW&Tの場所にきたら、糸を手前に持っていき、次の目を右針にすべり目。手前に持ってきた糸をすべった目の左から回すように後ろに持っていき、すべった目をまた左針に戻す。編地を返し、そのまま編み進める。

裏側でのW&T: パターン内でW&Tの場所にきたら、糸を向こう側に持っていき、次の目を右針にすべり目。向こう側に持っていった糸をすべった目の左から回すように手前に持っていき、すべった目を また左針に戻す。編地を返し、そのまま編み進める。

表側での段消し: ラップされた目の手前まで編む。ラップされた目を右針へ移し、左針を使って目の下に巻き付いた目を取る。この2目を2目一度する。

裏側での段消し: ラップされた目の手前まで編む。ラップされた目を右針へ移し、左針を使って目の下に巻き付いた目を取る。この2目をねじり目の裏2目一度する。

Magic loop

長い輪針で小さな輪を編む技法。柔らかいコードの輪針が必要。まず輪針に掛かっている目を均等に分け、目と目の間からコードを引き出す。両針が右側にくるよう揃えて持ち、後ろ側の針を引張ってコードを引き出す。その針を使い手前の針に掛かっている目を編んでいく。編み終わった後は、編地を返し、コードを引張り手前の針先に目がくるようにする。これを繰返す。